AMOK BOOKS
KALEIDOSCOPIC
CREATURES BOOK 1

I0476959

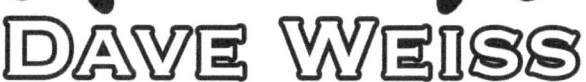

DAVE WEISS

AMOKBOOKS, MOHRSVILLE, PA

DWEISSCREATIVE.COM

Why Kaleidoscopics?

Some people call them Mandalas, but I'm just not comfortable with that. Mandalas are sometimes associated with eastern religious rituals and that's not the direction I'm taking. To me these pieces are a departure from what I usually do. They are created in pieces and cut together into the images you see before you and while I have some idea what the final piece will look like, it is often a very pleasant surprise. It's as if the piece is seen through that favorite childhood toy, a kaleidoscope.

Why Creatures?

I have always loved to draw creatures, from my earliest childhood, to my time freelancing for a licensee of the *Teenage Mutant Ninja Turtles*, to my days doing children's coloring books to my web comic *Creacher*. The reasons are multiple. First of all, many of them do not exist in the real world, so I can literally create anything I want. Additionally, in cartooning there is often sensitivity. People are often sensitive to the way they are portrayed. Controversy can keep people from hearing your message. Creatures look like no one and, as a result, can speak to everyone. What's not to love?

I think of my work on these pages as a kind of artistic jam session—giving my creativity wings and letting it soar. It is my hope that you, the colorist, will do the same. There is no right or wrong way to interpret these, only your way. Have fun with them. Get your materials out and let your creativity take flight. Whether you are coloring just to relax or you're trying to recapture your creativity, know this. You are creative and you are an artist. Pablo Picasso once said, "All children are artists, the problem is to remain one as one grows up."

Welcome back to art. The sky's the limit! Have fun!

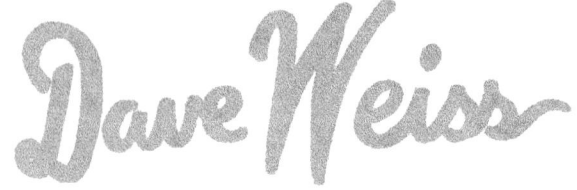

Published Mohrsville, Pennsylvania, by David C. Weiss for AMOK Books. AMOK Books, AMOKArts and A.M.O.K. Arts Ministry Outreach for the Kingdom are trademarks of David C. Weiss

Illustrations by David C. Weiss, AMOKArts.com

ISBN-13: 978-1522980162
ISBN-10: 1522980164

Library of Congress Cataloging-in Publication Data

Weiss, David C., 1963-
Kaleidoscopic Creatures: Book 1, 50 Images to Color by David C. Weiss

ISBN
1. Weiss, David C., 1963- 2. Art
3. Coloring

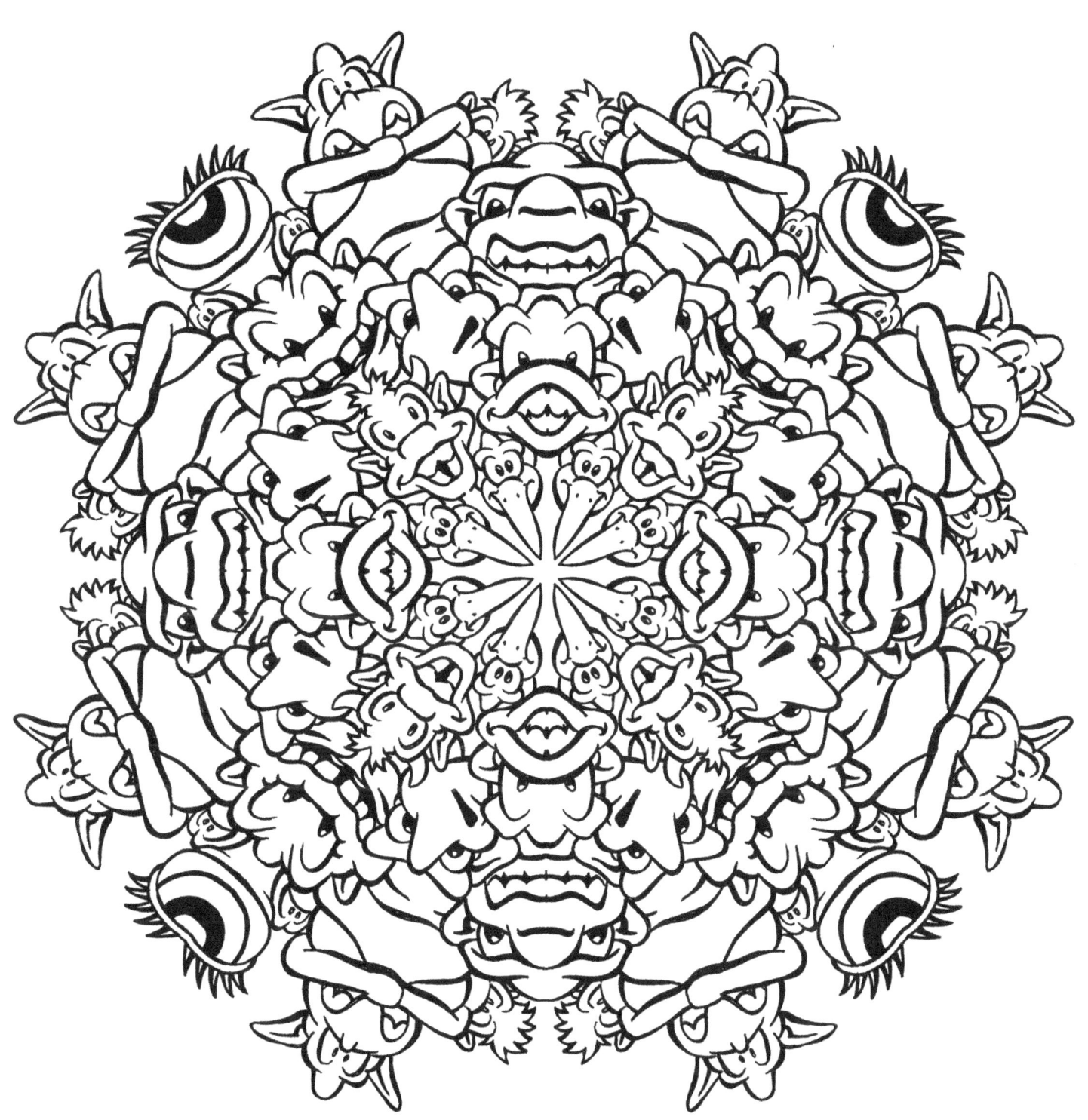

Dave Weiss

Kaleidoscopic Creatures Book 1
"Creature Club"

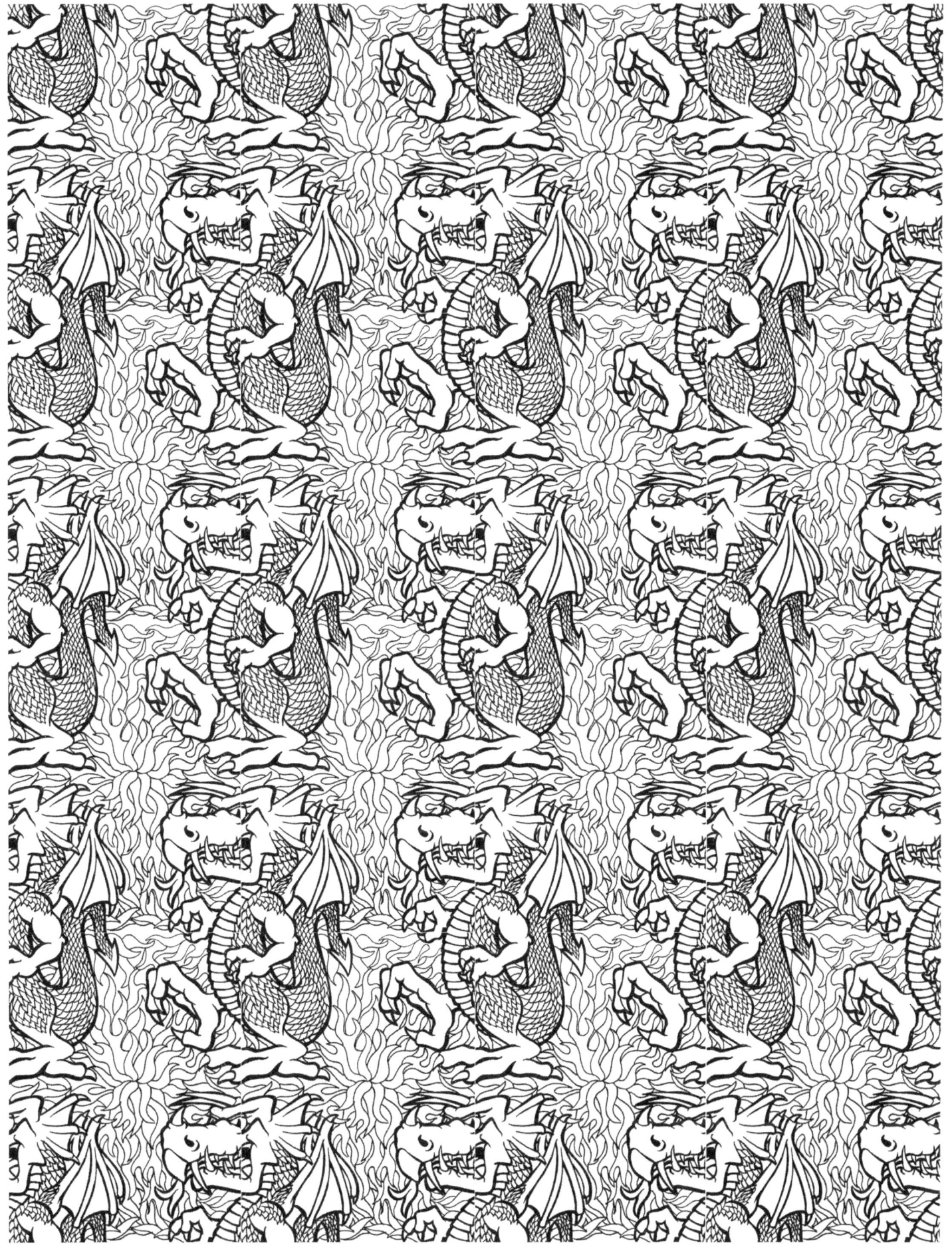

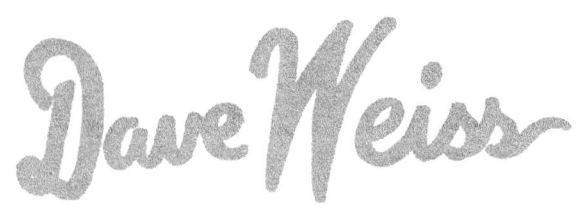

Kaleidoscopic Creatures Book 1
"Dragon Fire"

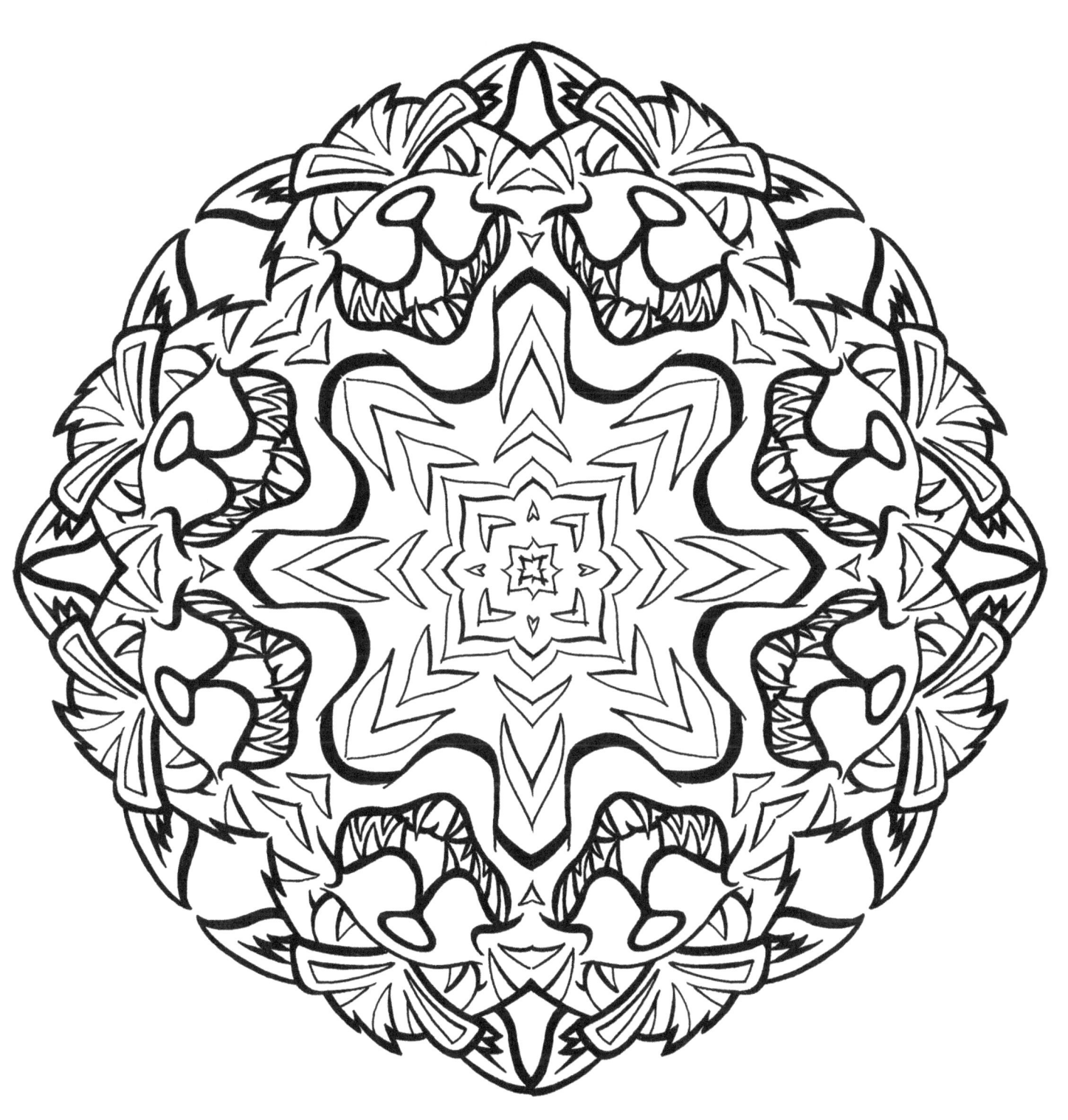

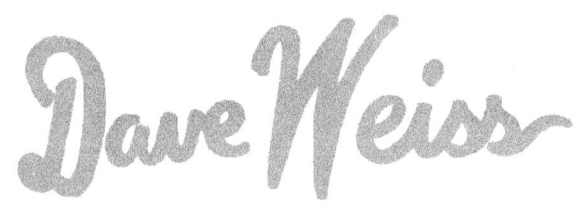

Kaleidoscopic Creatures Book 1
"Cheshire"

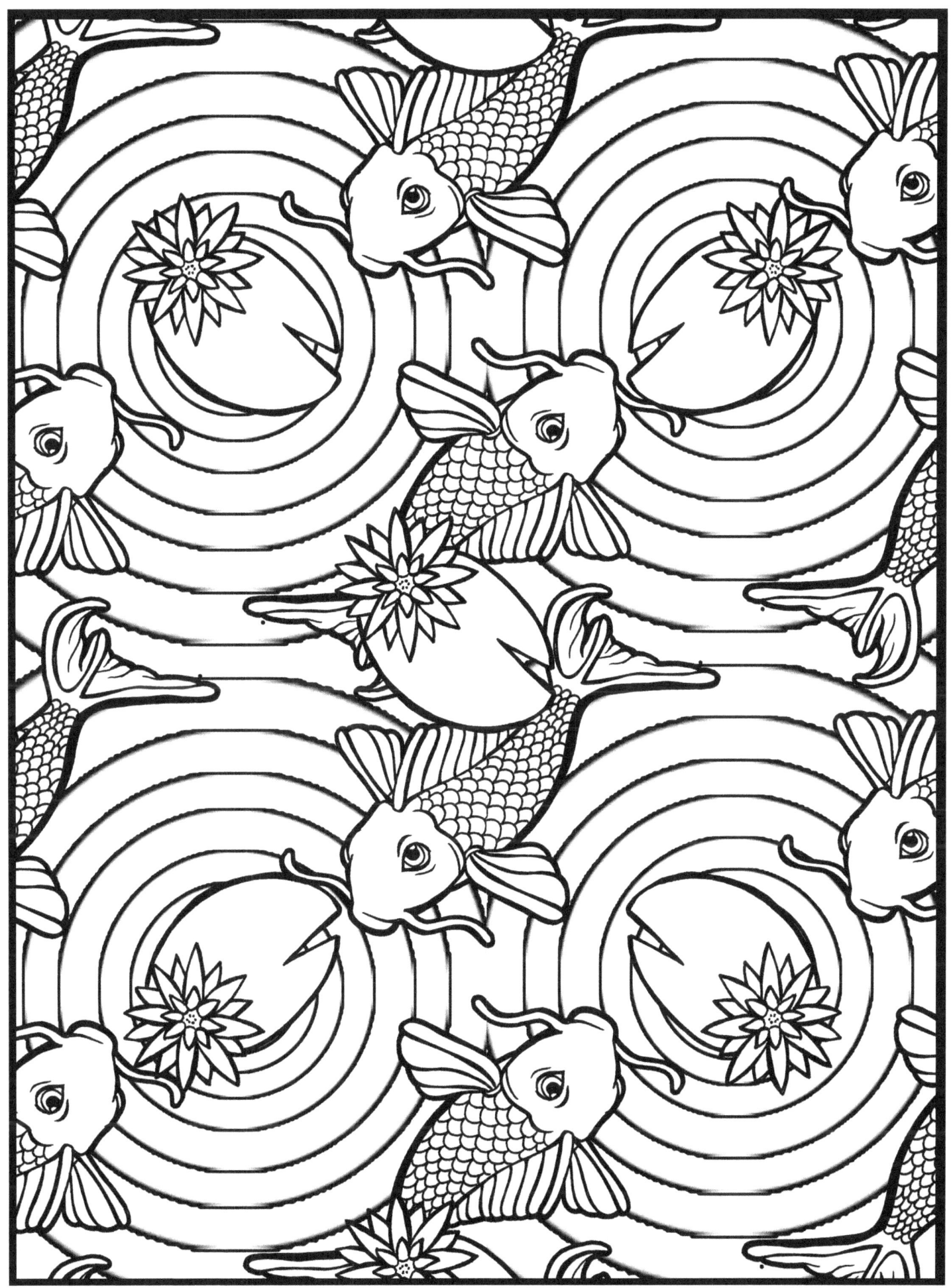

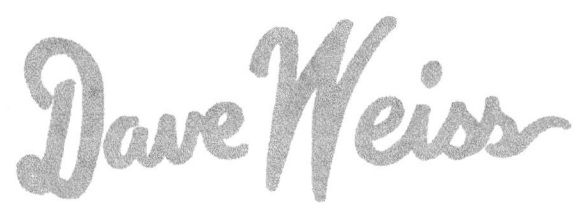

Kaleidoscopic Creatures Book 1
"Koi Pond"

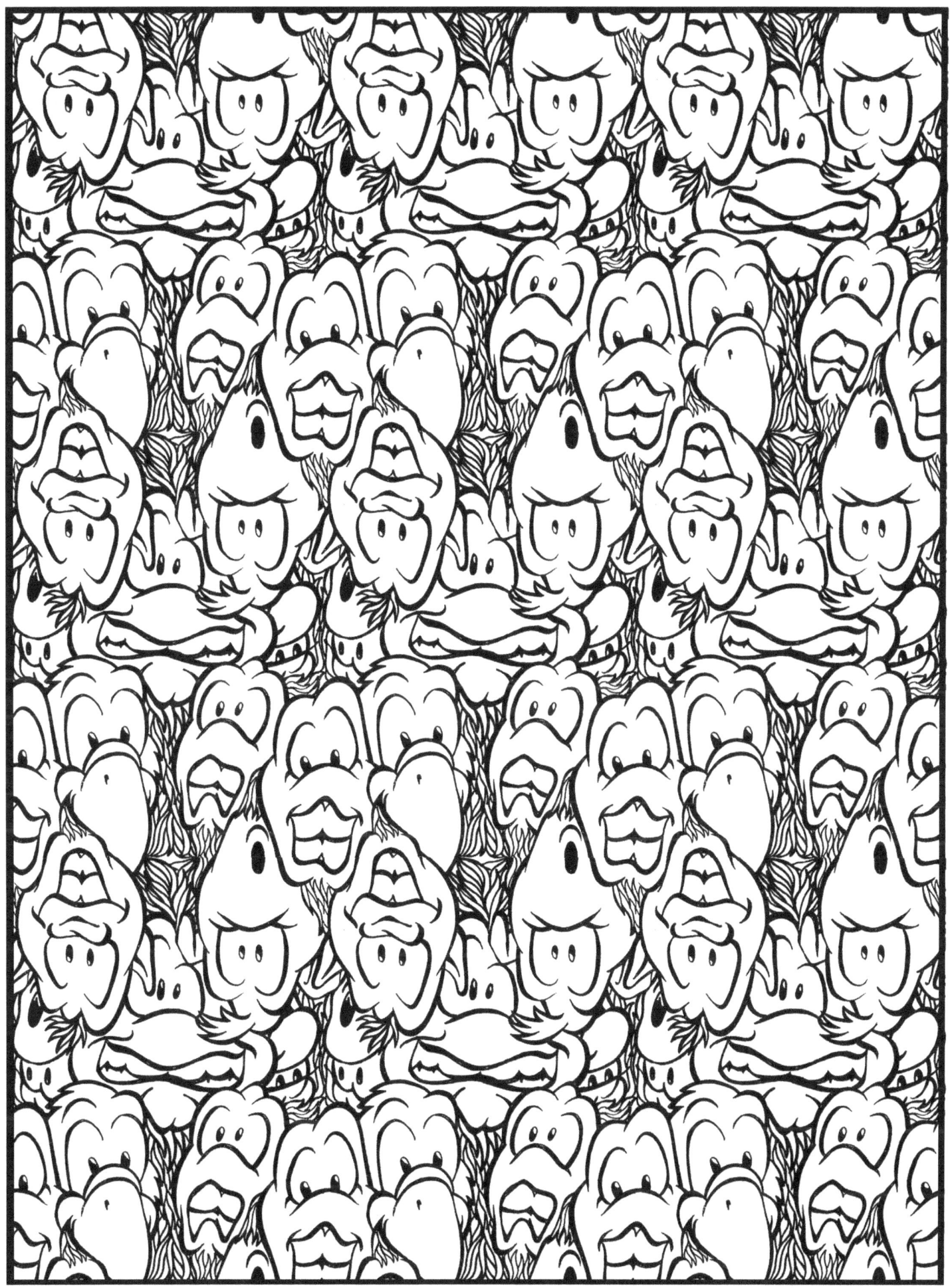

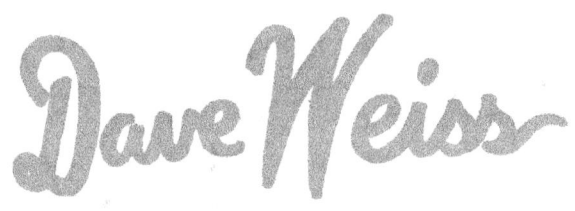

Kaleidoscopic Creatures Book 1
"Sea of Faces"

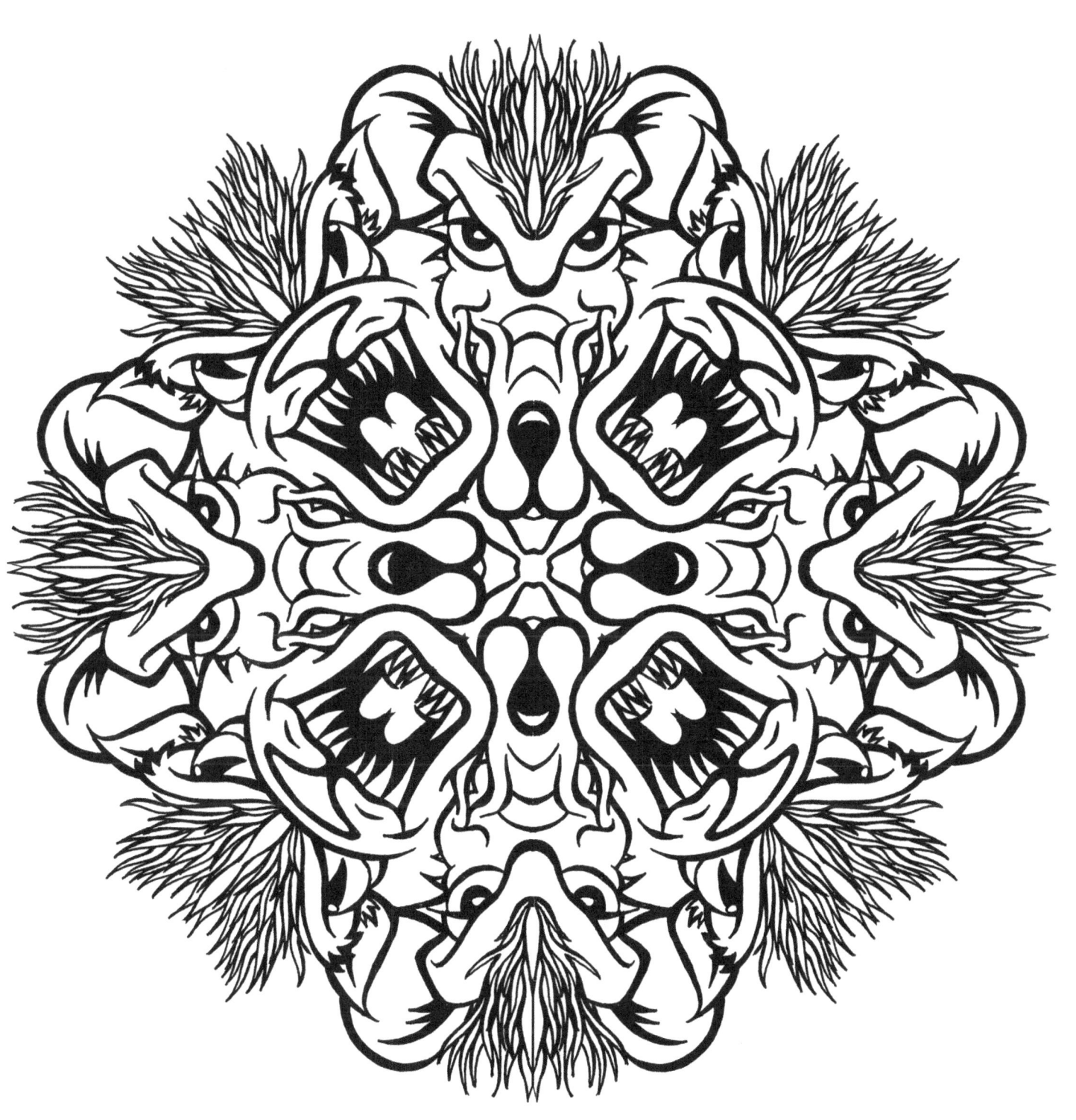

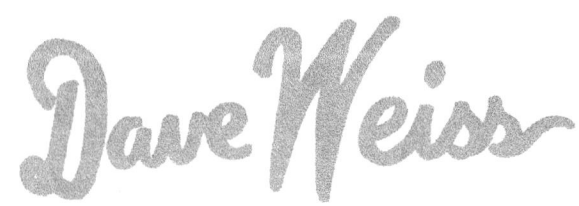

Kaleidoscopic Creatures Book 1
"Cats and Rats"

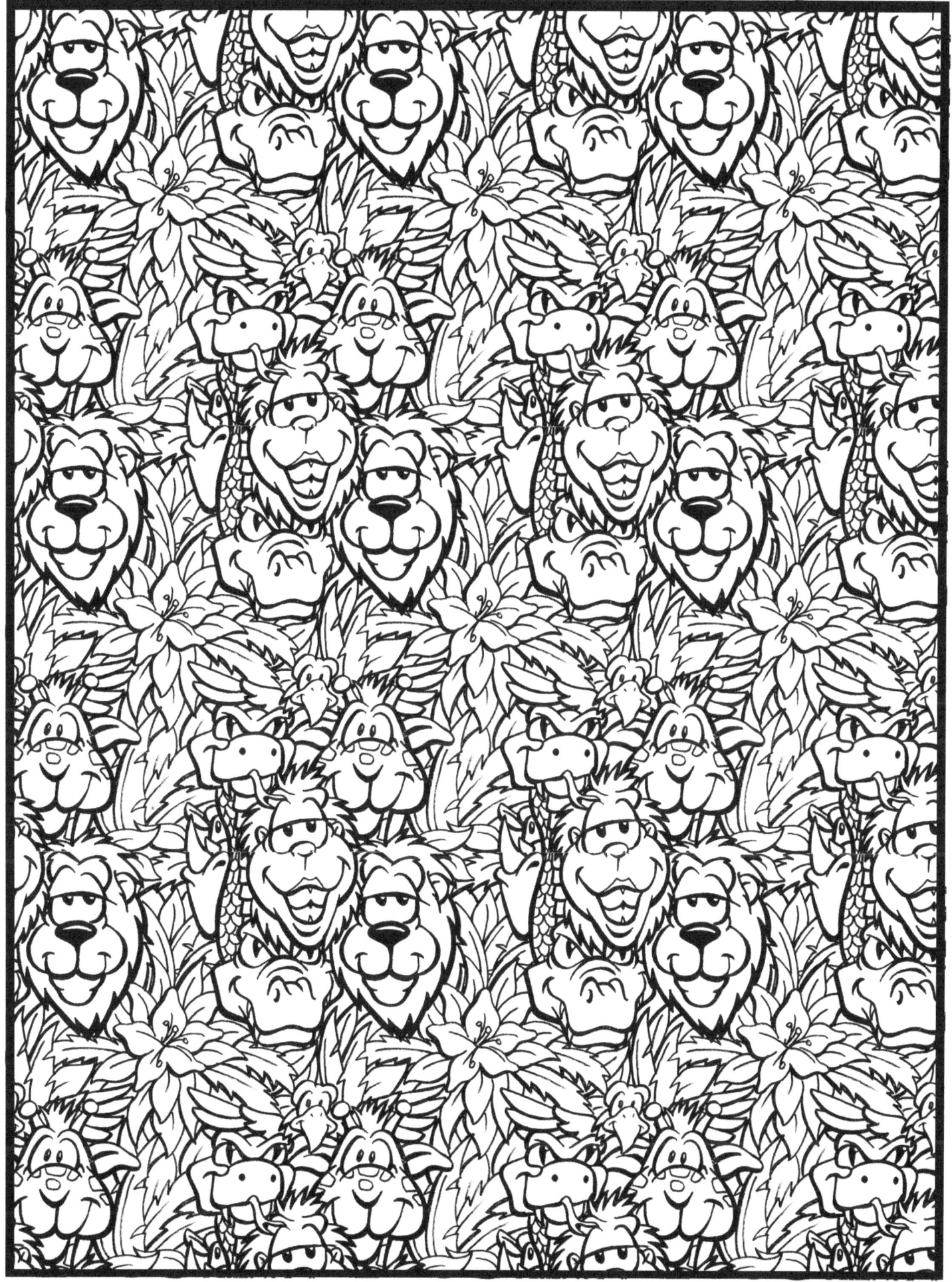

Dave Weiss

Kaleidoscopic Creatures Book 1
"It's a Jungle Out There"

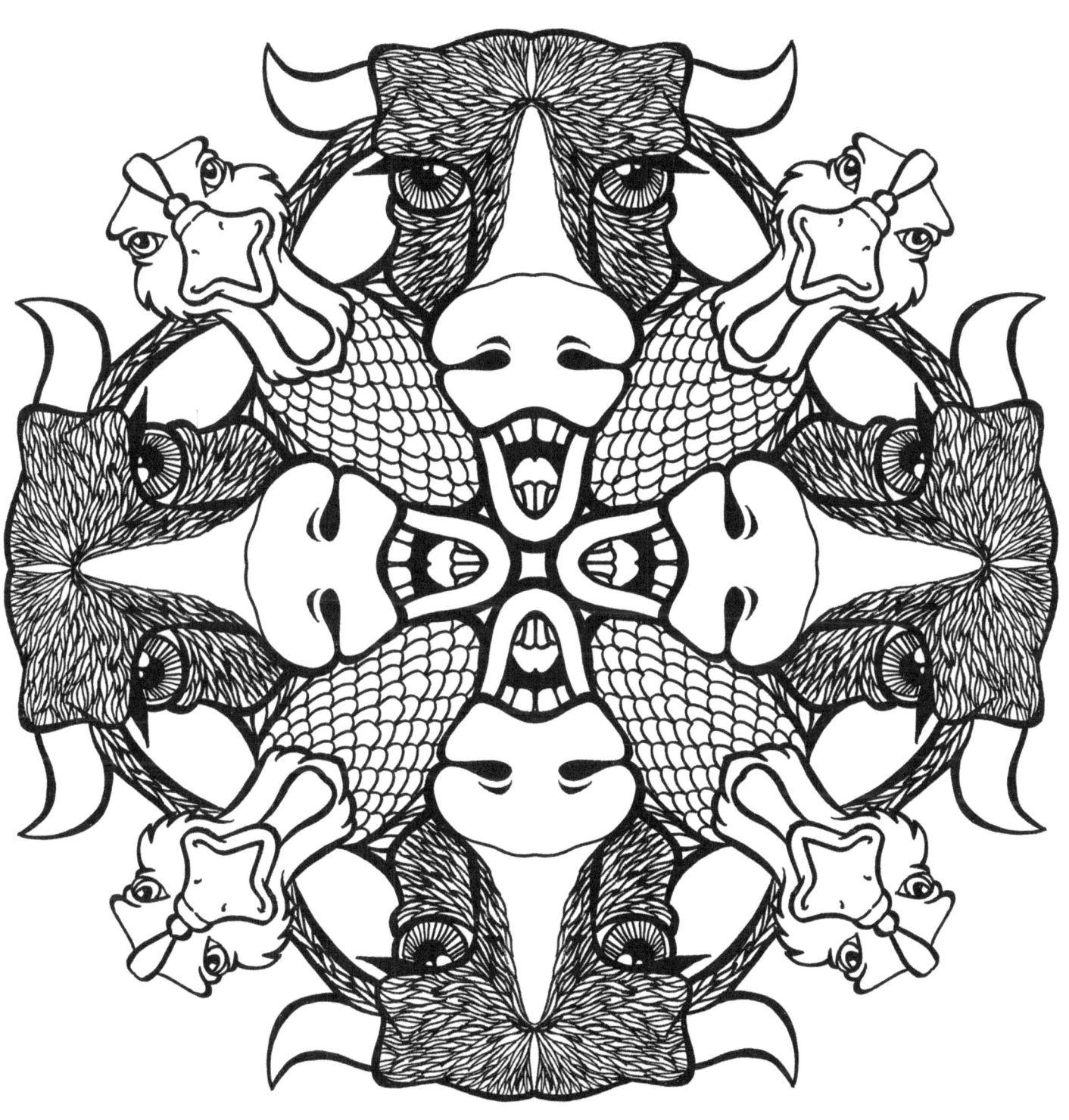

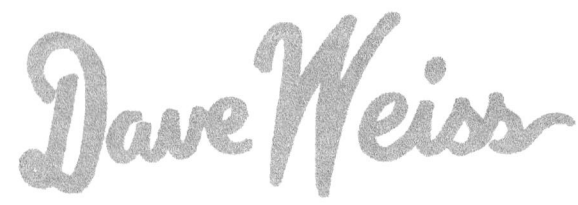

Kaleidoscopic Creatures Book 1
"Down On the Farm"

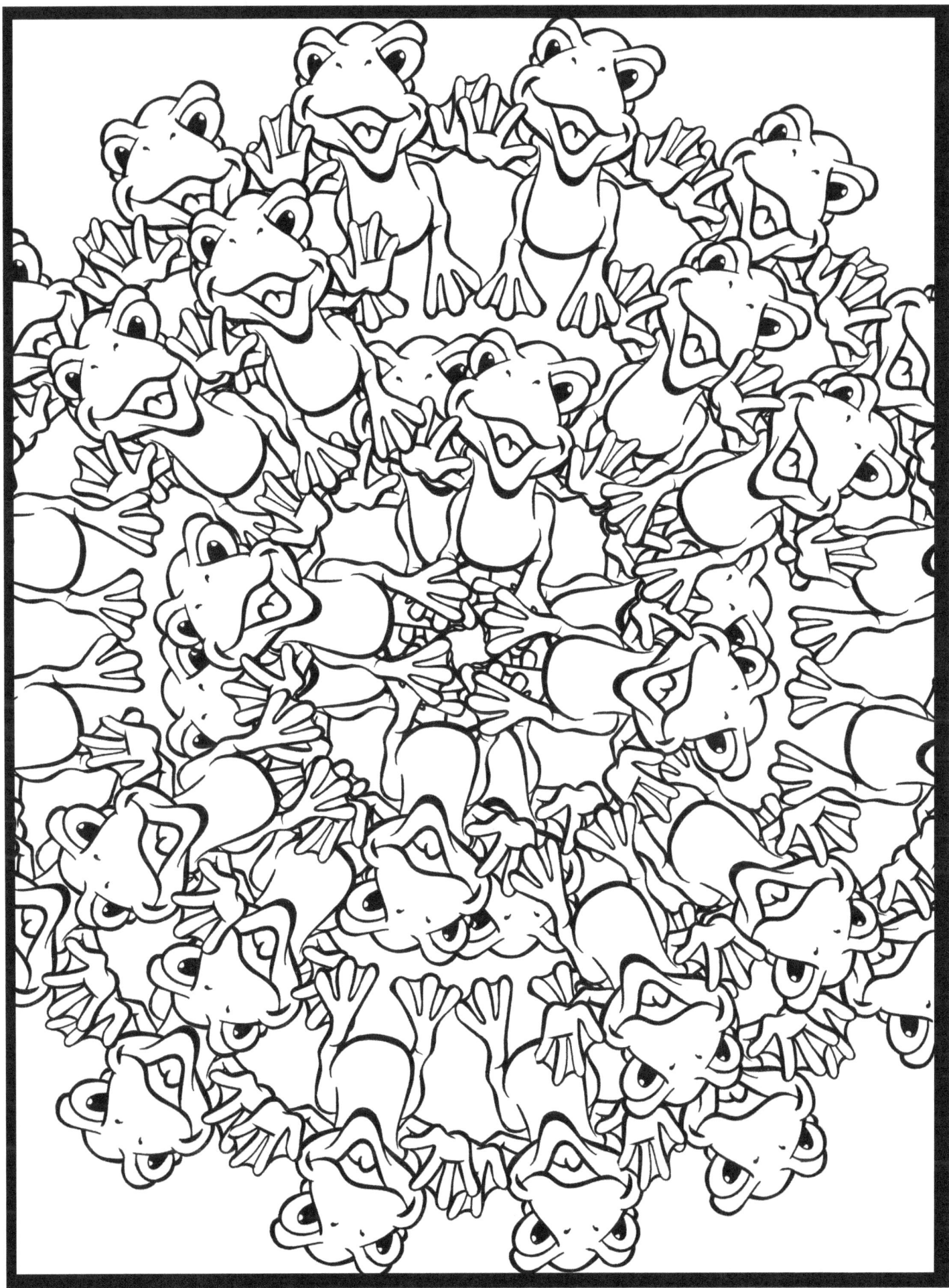

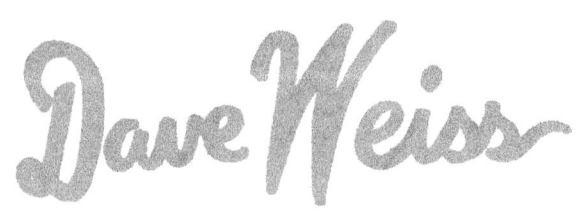

Kaleidoscopic Creatures Book 1
"Froggin' Out"

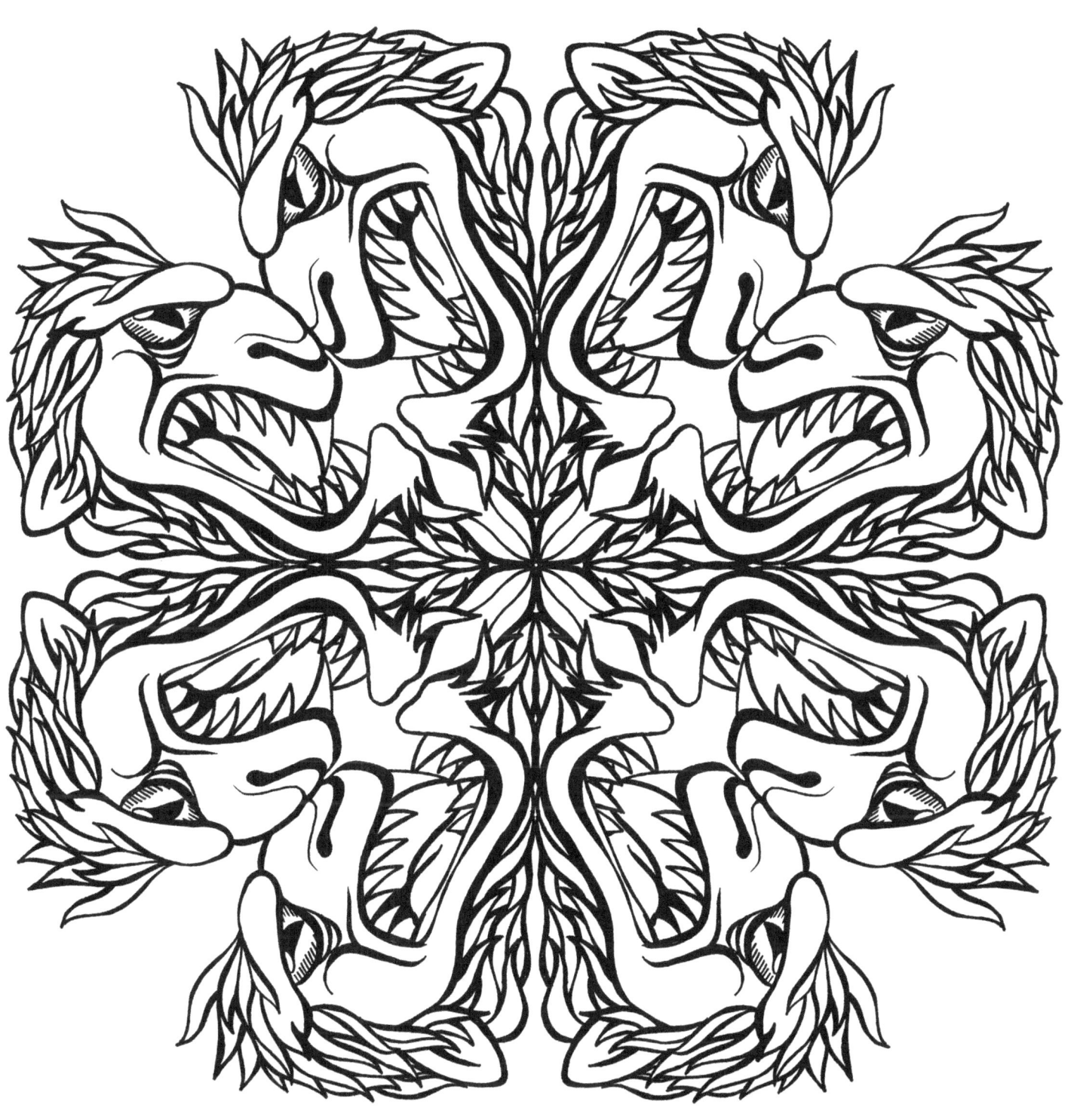

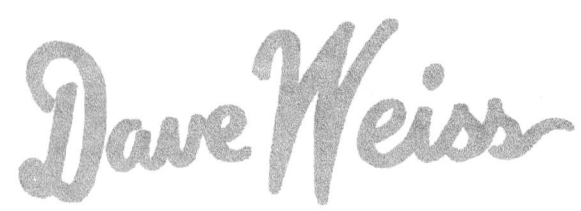

Kaleidoscopic Creatures Book 1
"Pride Rears Its Head"

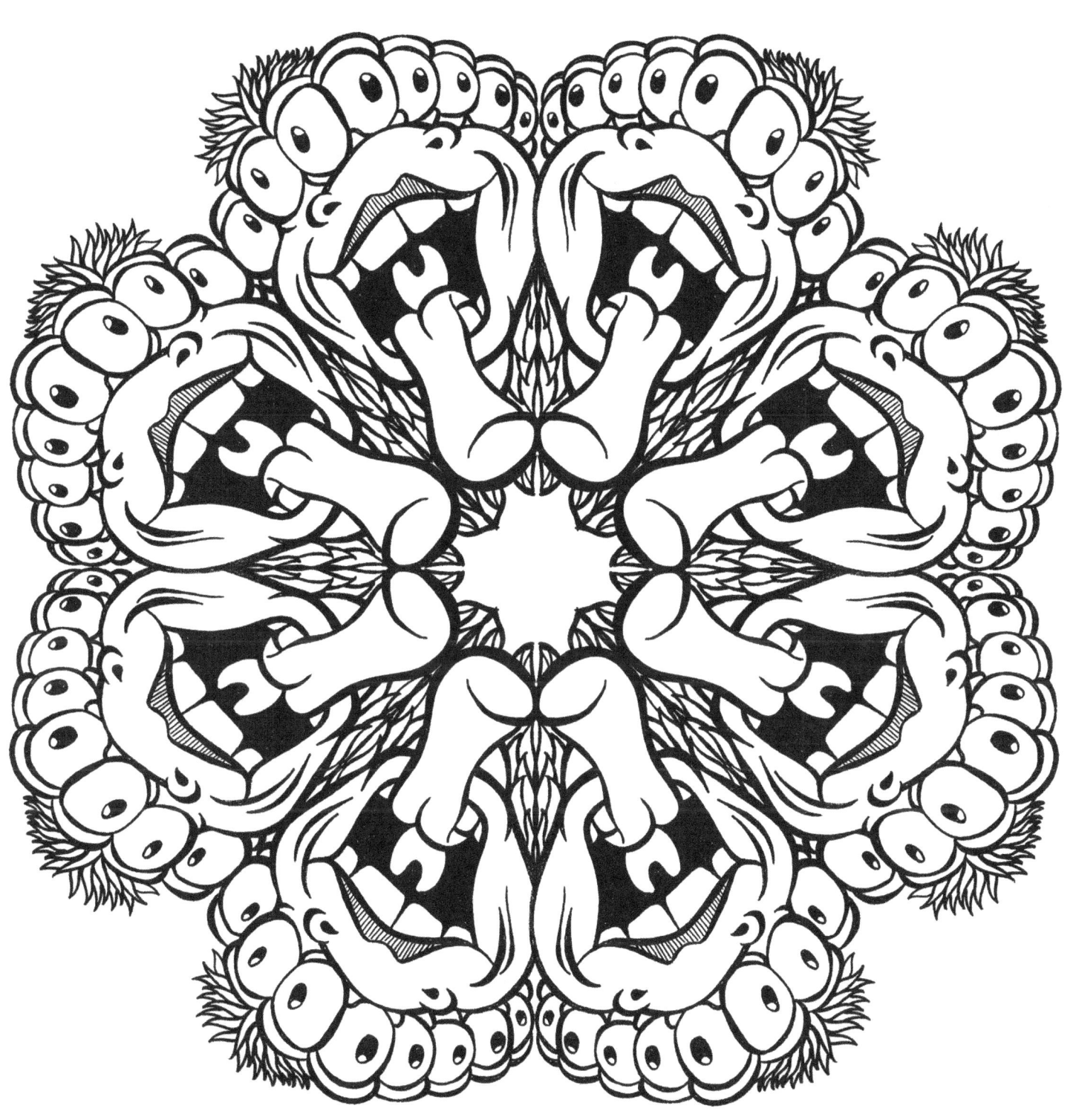

Dave Weiss

Kaleidoscopic Creatures Book 1
"64 Eyes"

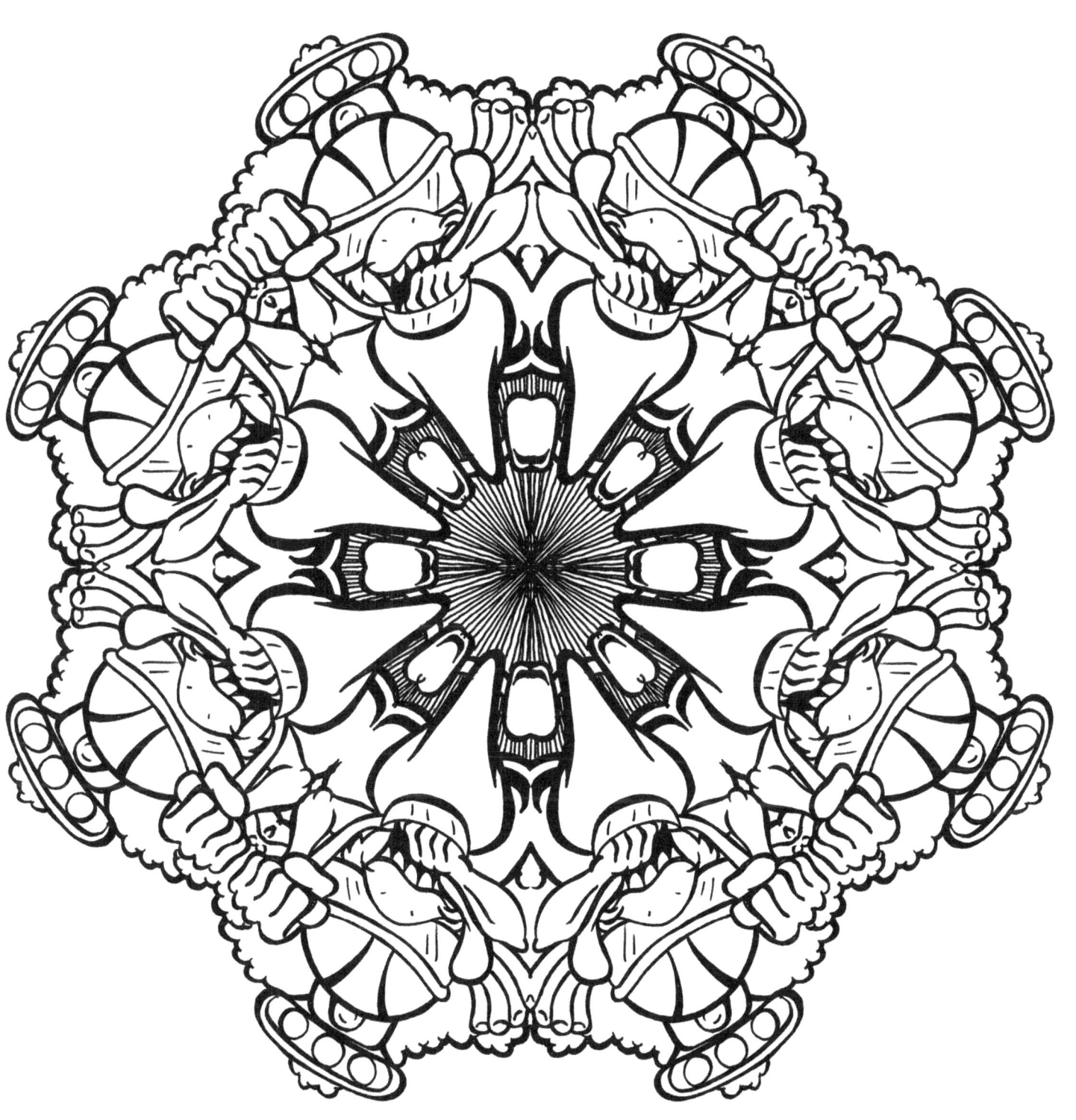

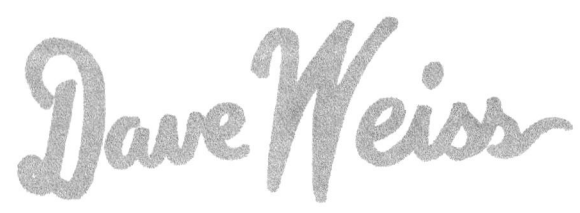

Kaleidoscopic Creatures Book 1
"Life's a Drag"

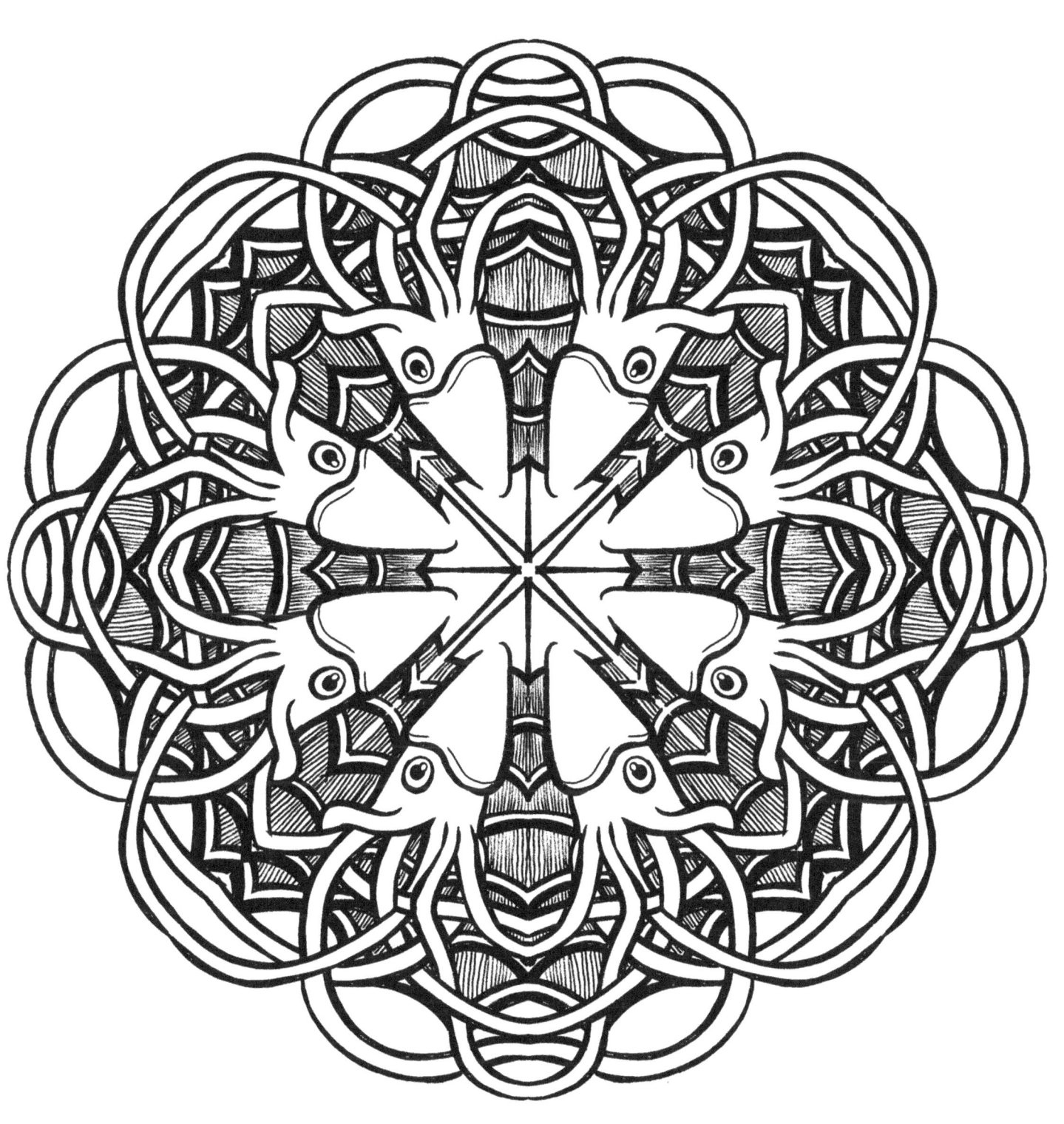

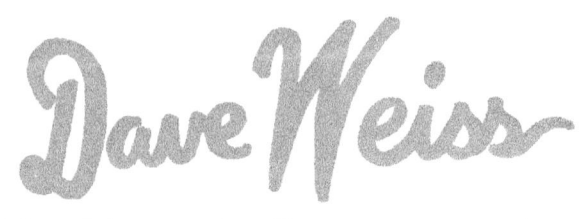

Kaleidoscopic Creatures Book 1
"Squidtastic"

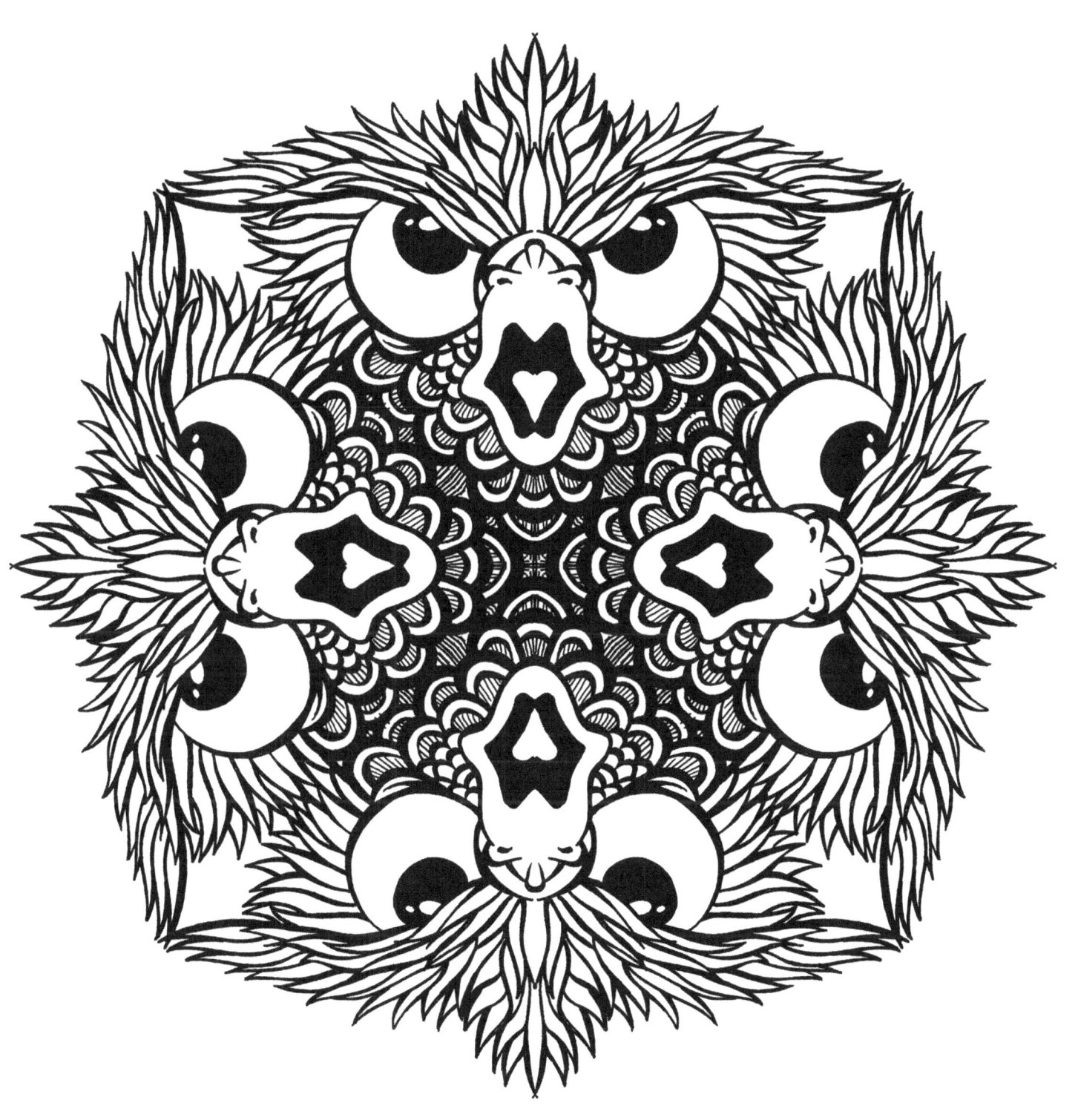

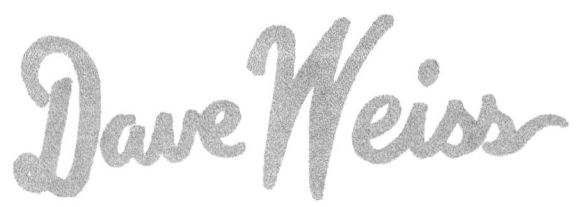

Kaleidoscopic Creatures Book 1
"Eyes of the Night"

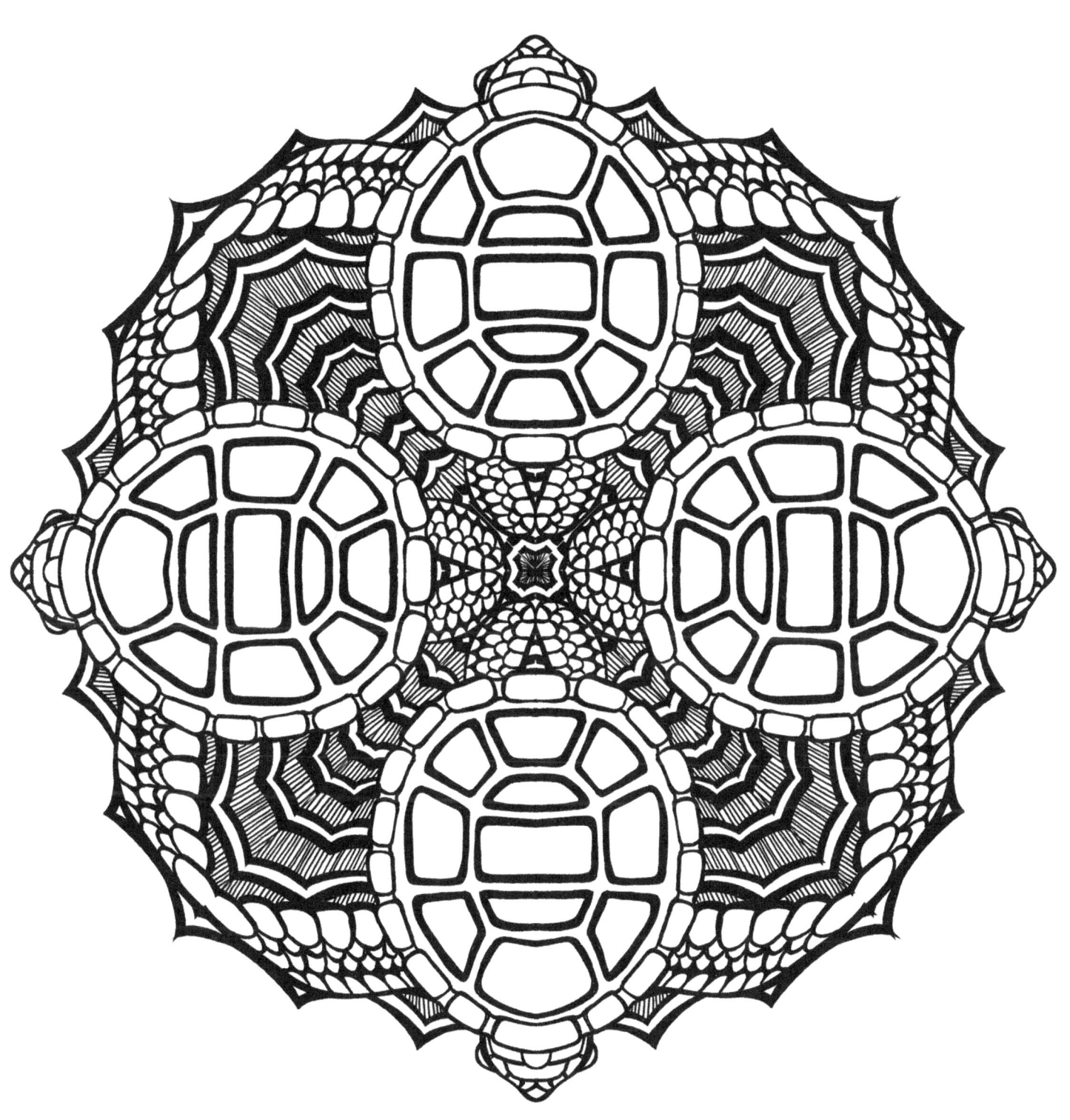

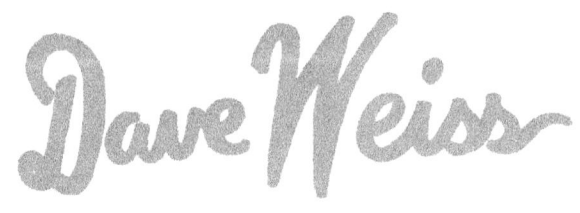

Kaleidoscopic Creatures Book 1
"Honu World"

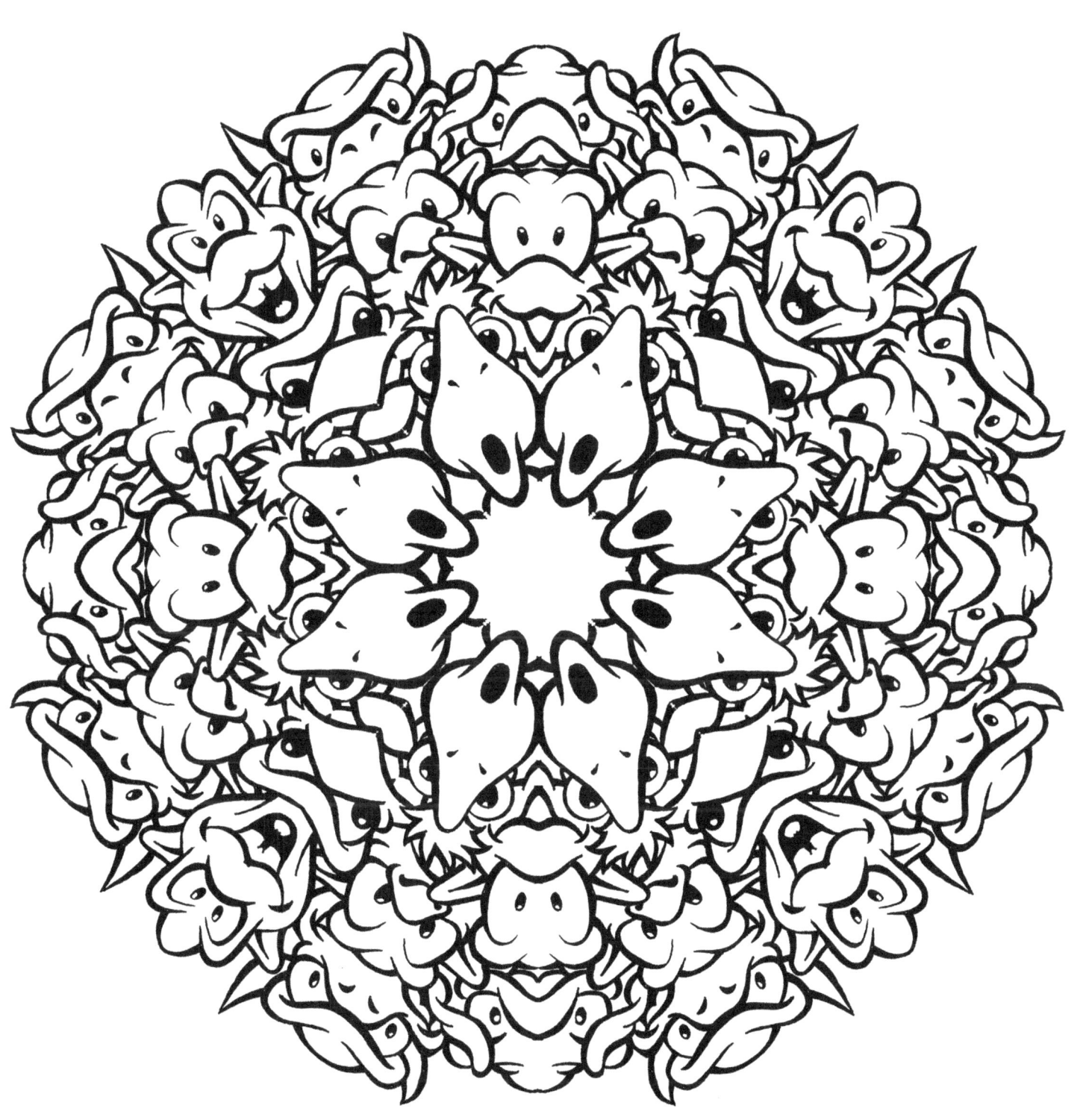

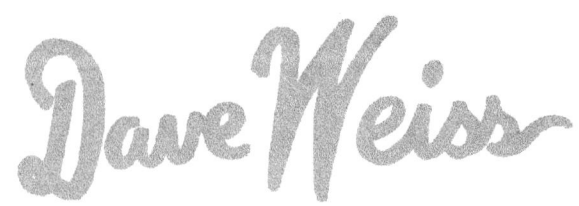

Kaleidoscopic Creatures Book 1
"Creature Cluster"

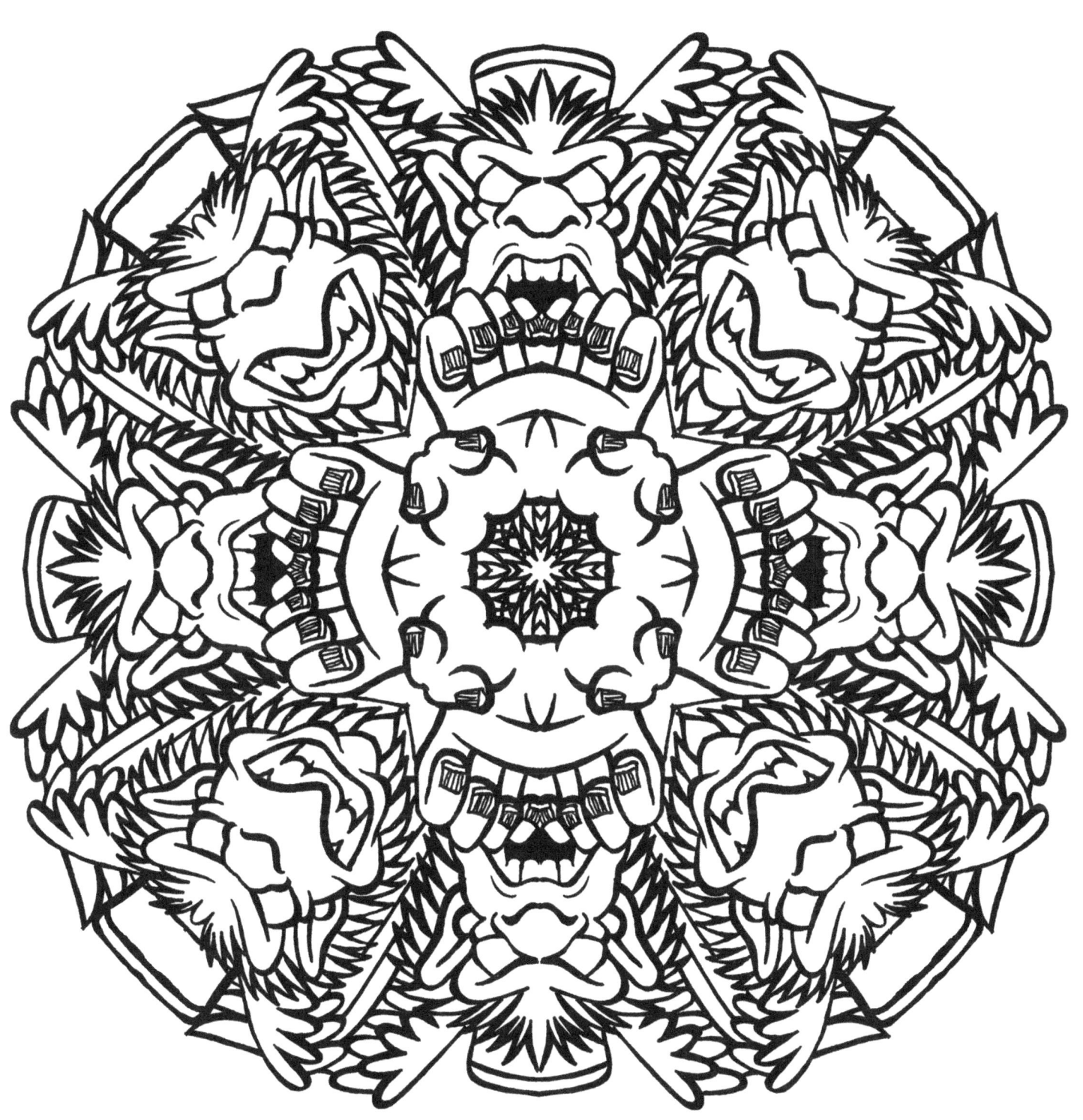

Dave Weiss

Kaleidoscopic Creatures Book 1
"Childhood Nightmare"

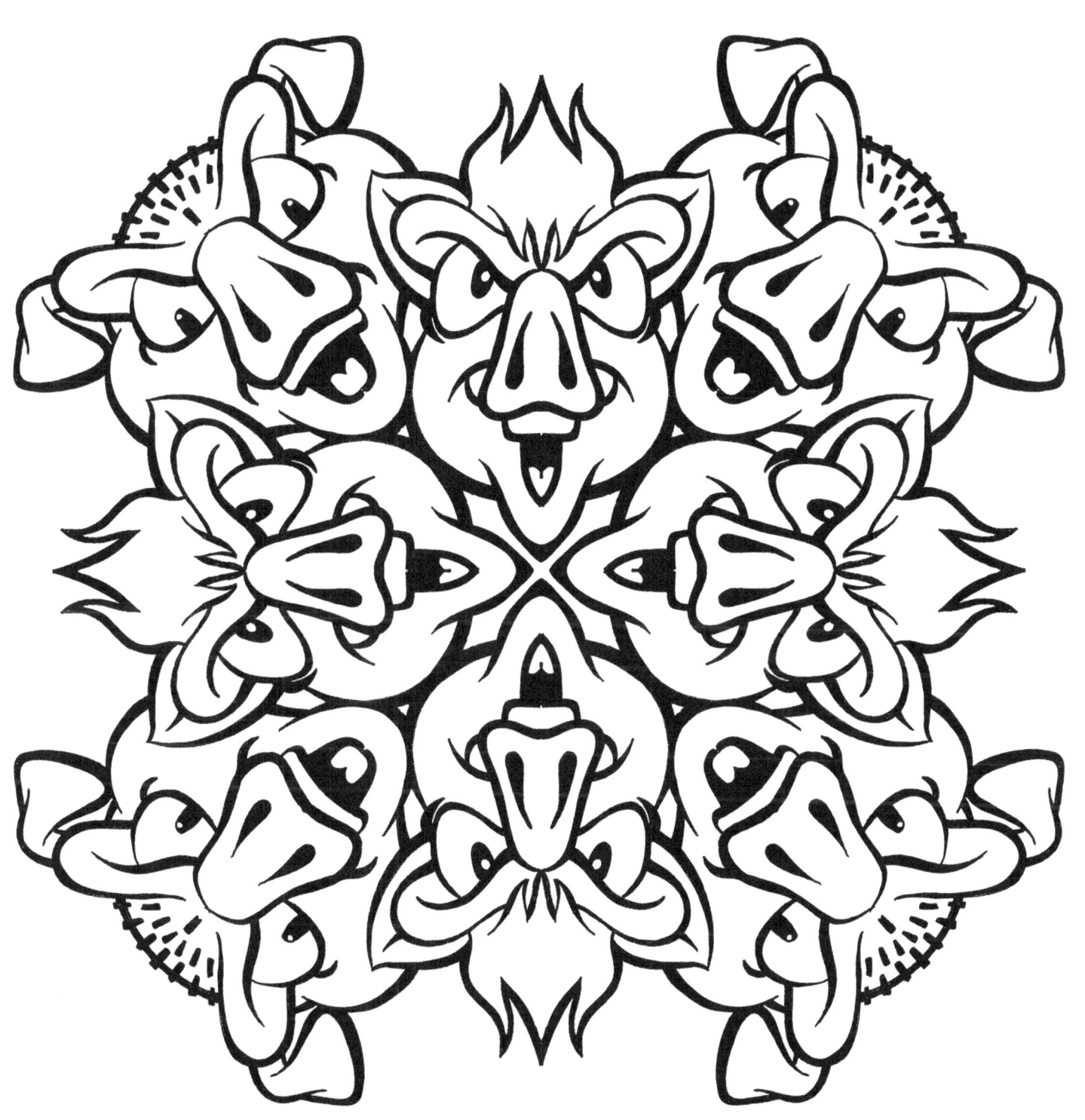

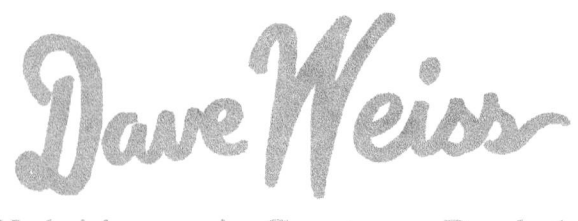

Kaleidoscopic Creatures Book 1
"Hog Wild"

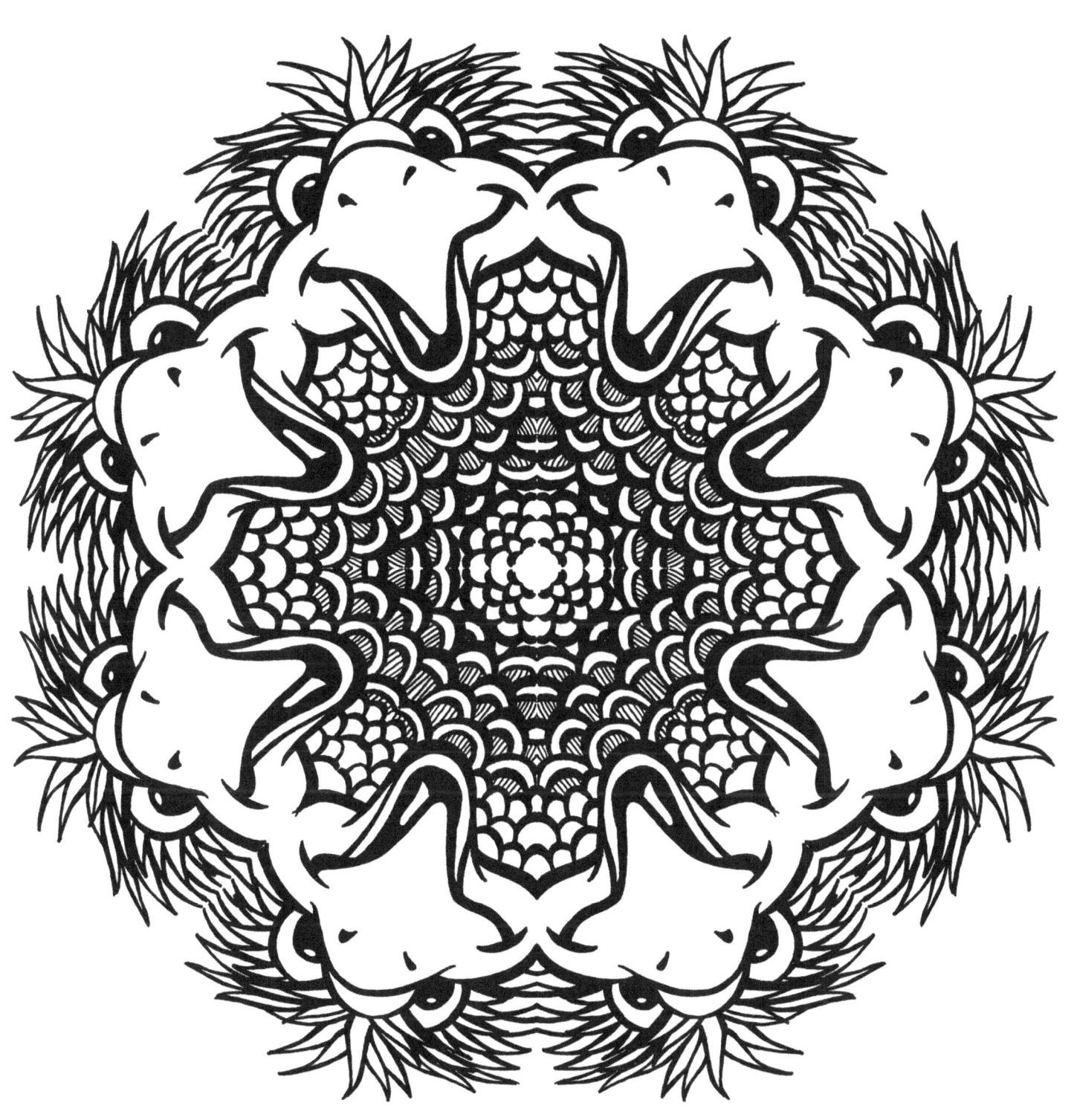

Dave Weiss

Kaleidoscopic Creatures Book 1
"Looney Bird"

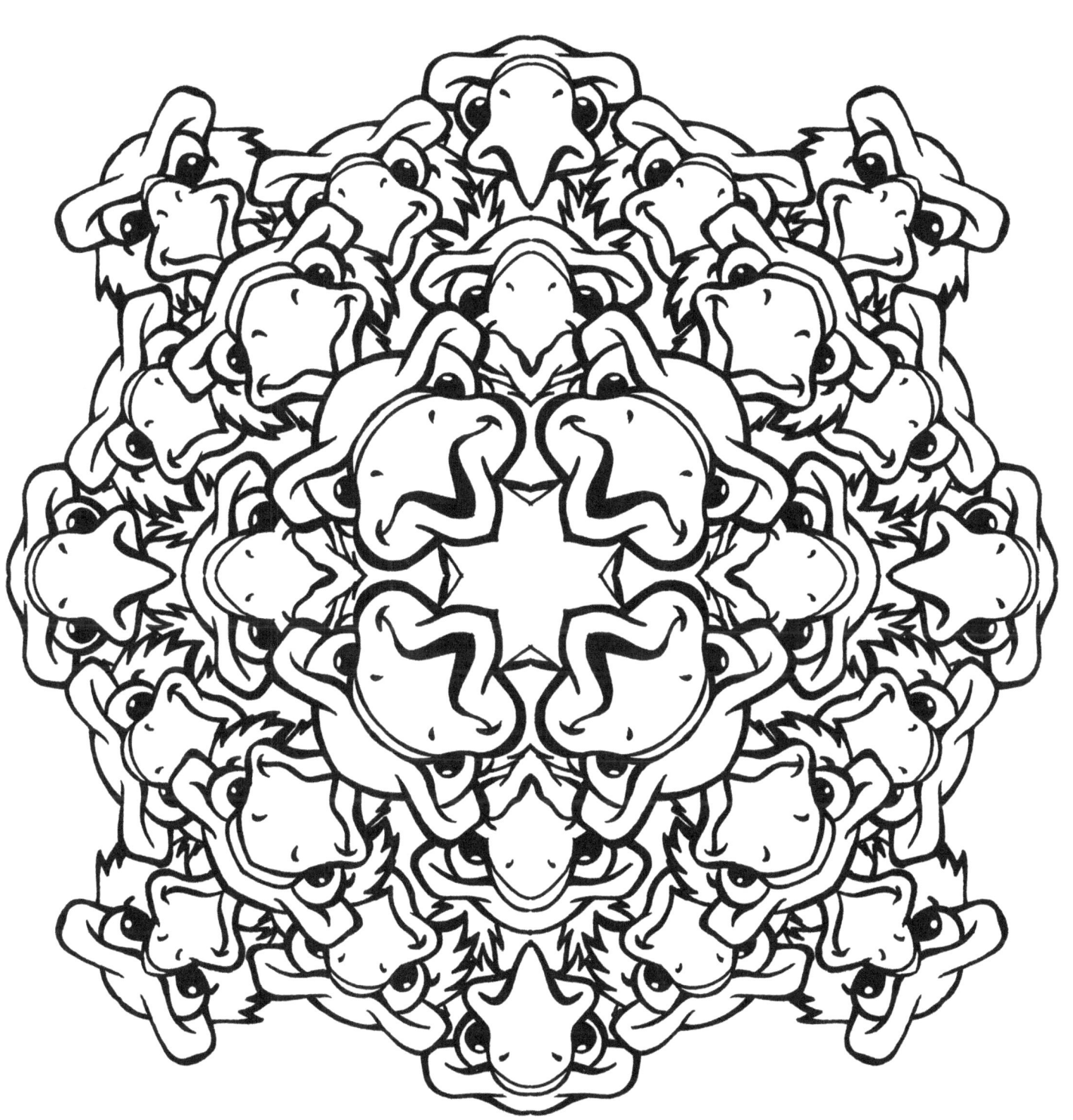

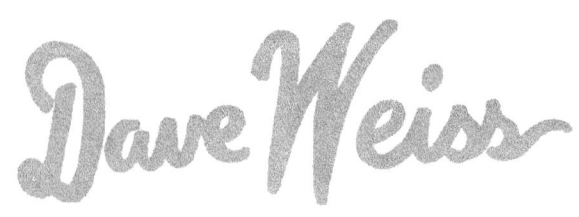

Kaleidoscopic Creatures Book 1
"Birds of Prey"

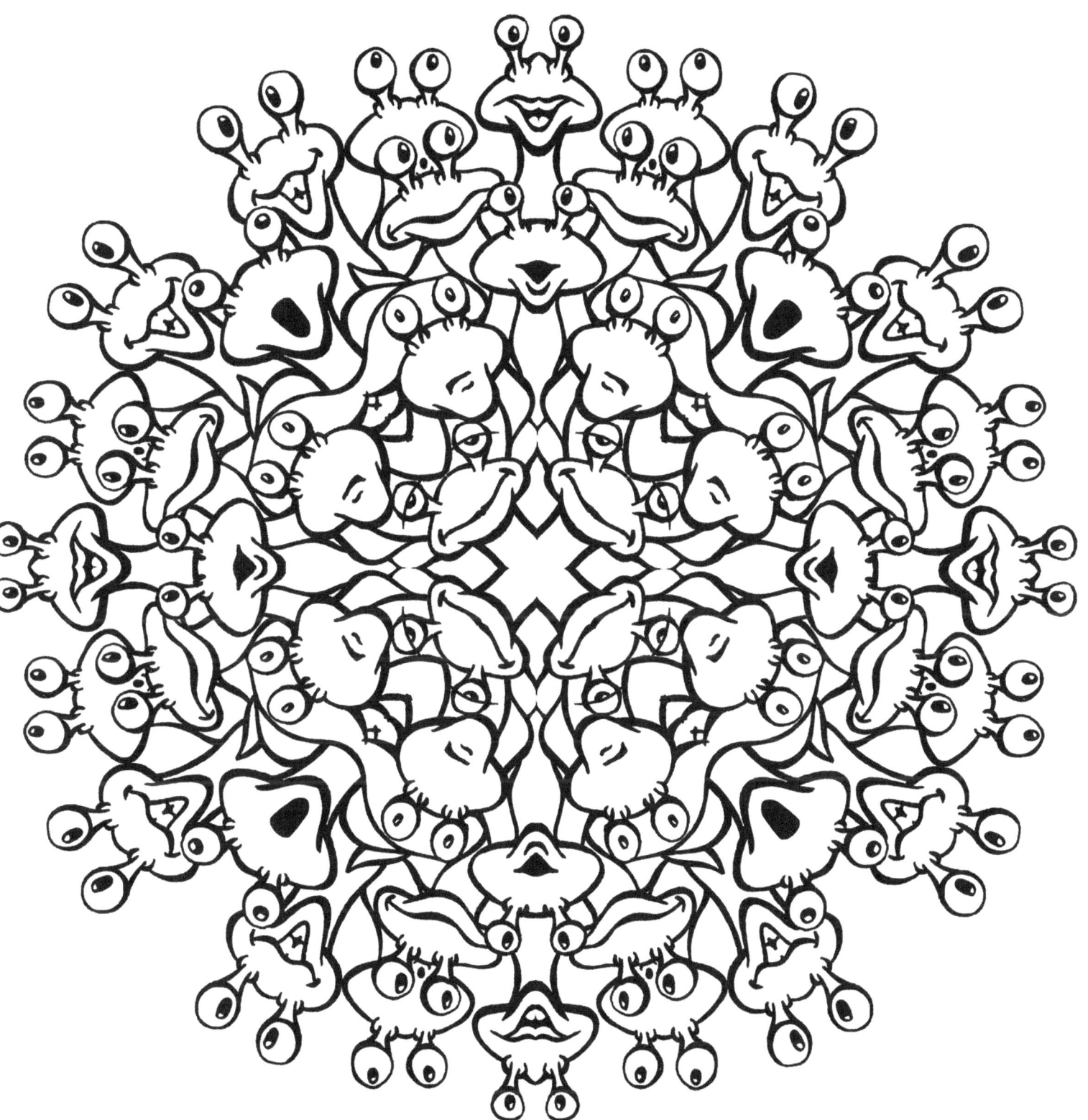

Dave Weiss

Kaleidoscopic Creatures Book 1
"Slug Fest"

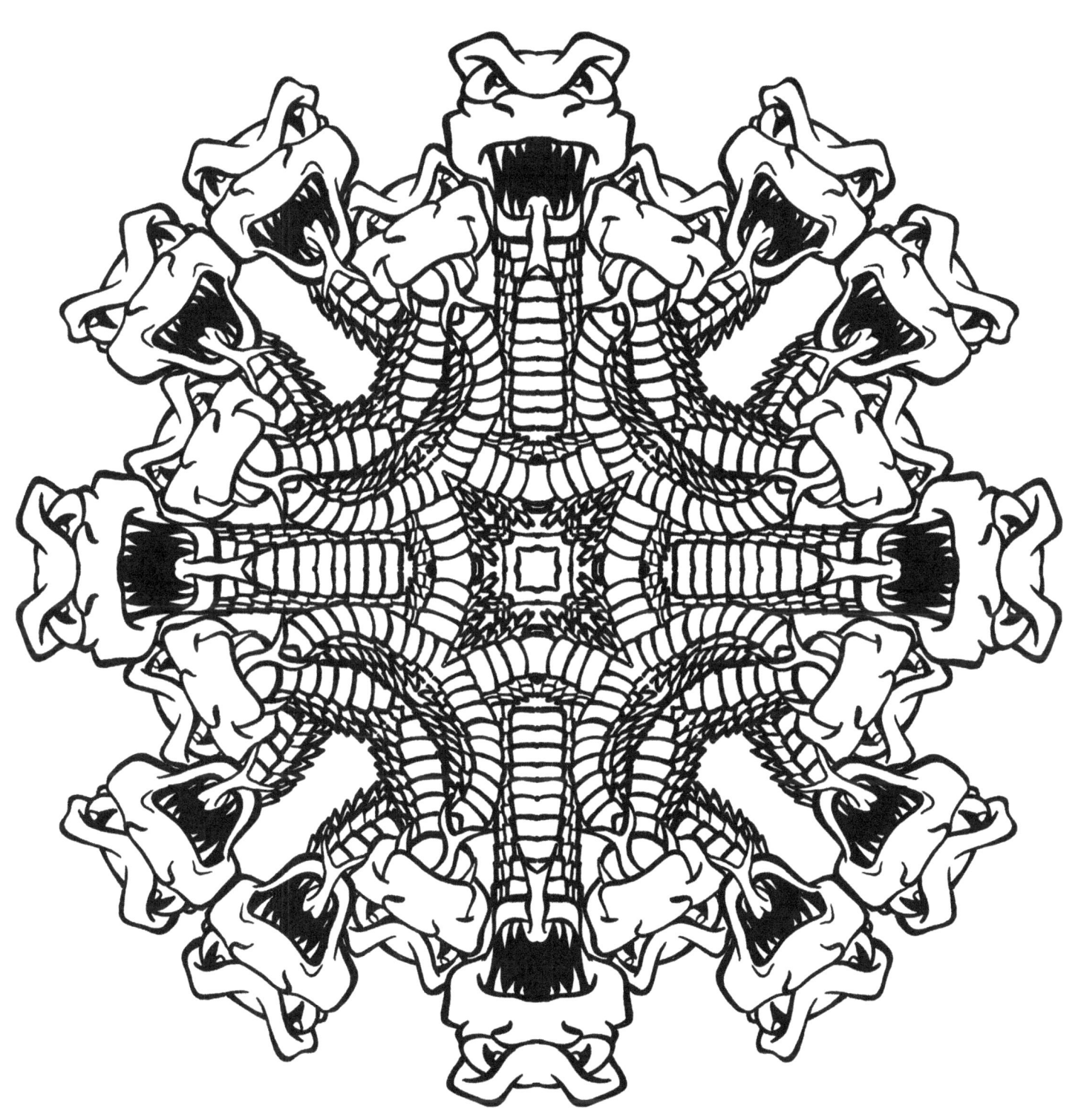

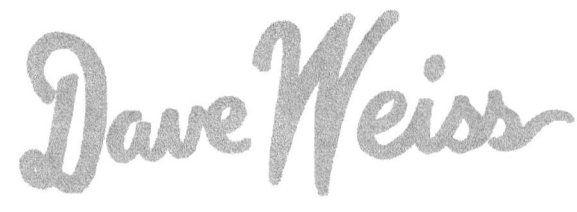

Dave Weiss

Kaleidoscopic Creatures Book 1
"Snake Pit"

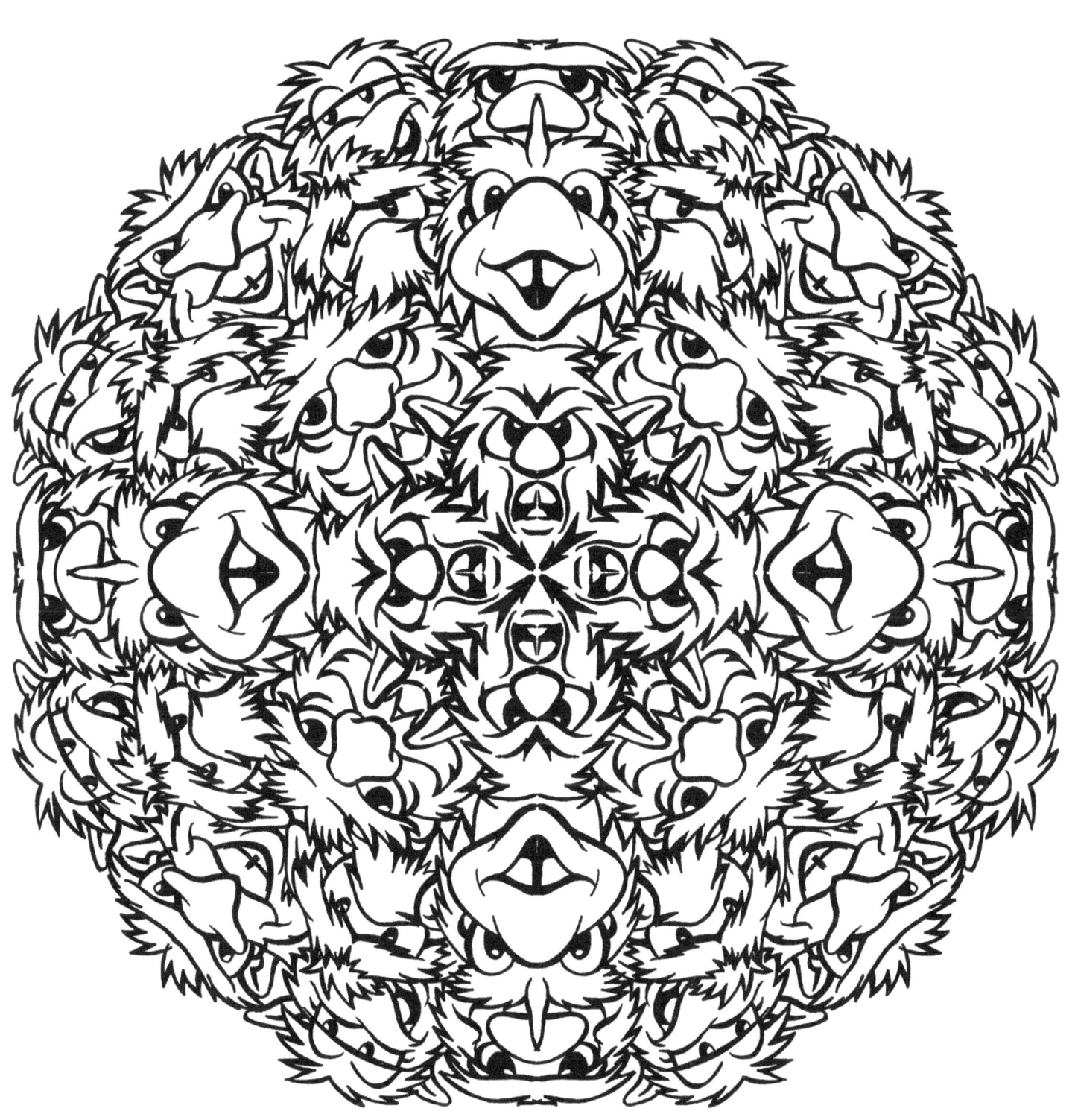

Dave Weiss

Kaleidoscopic Creatures Book 1
"Baddies"

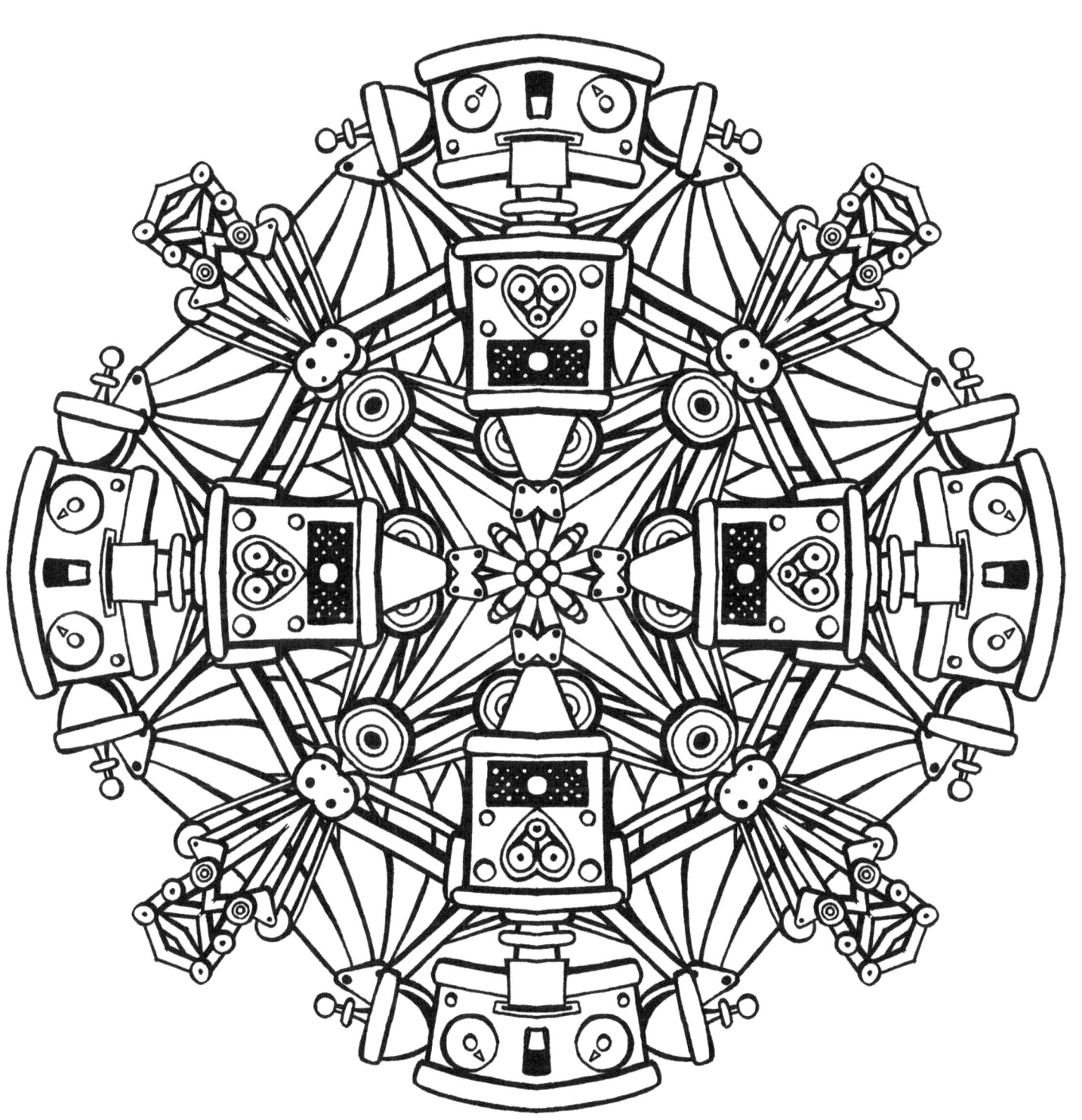

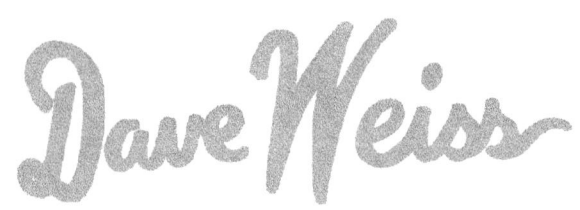

Kaleidoscopic Creatures Book 1
"Roboguru"

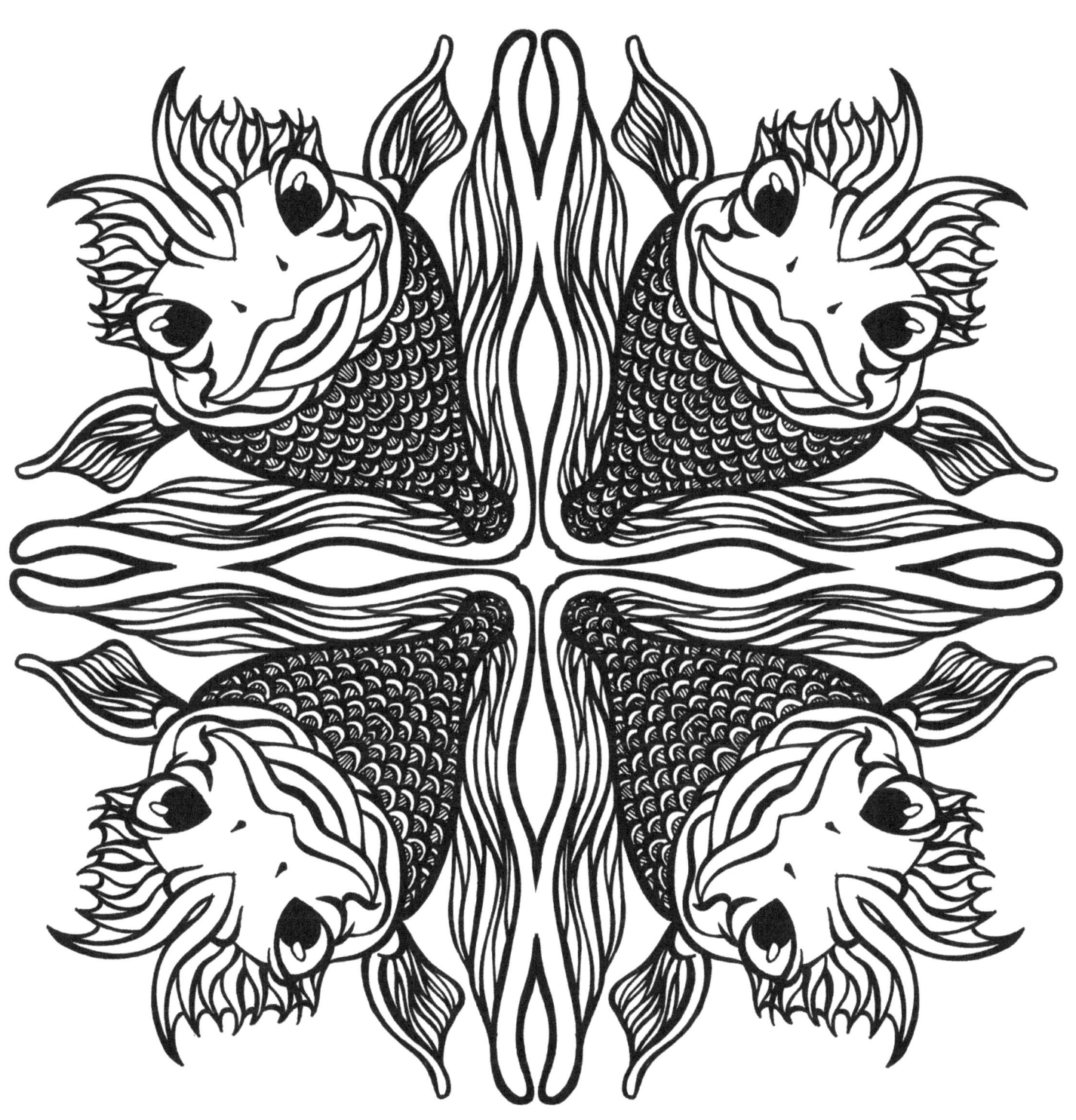

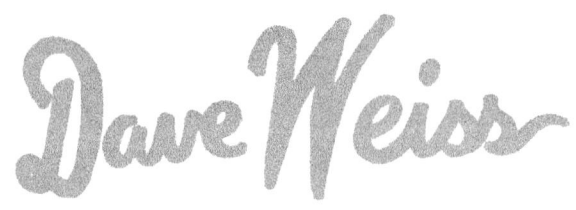

Kaleidoscopic Creatures Book 1
"Golden Goldie"

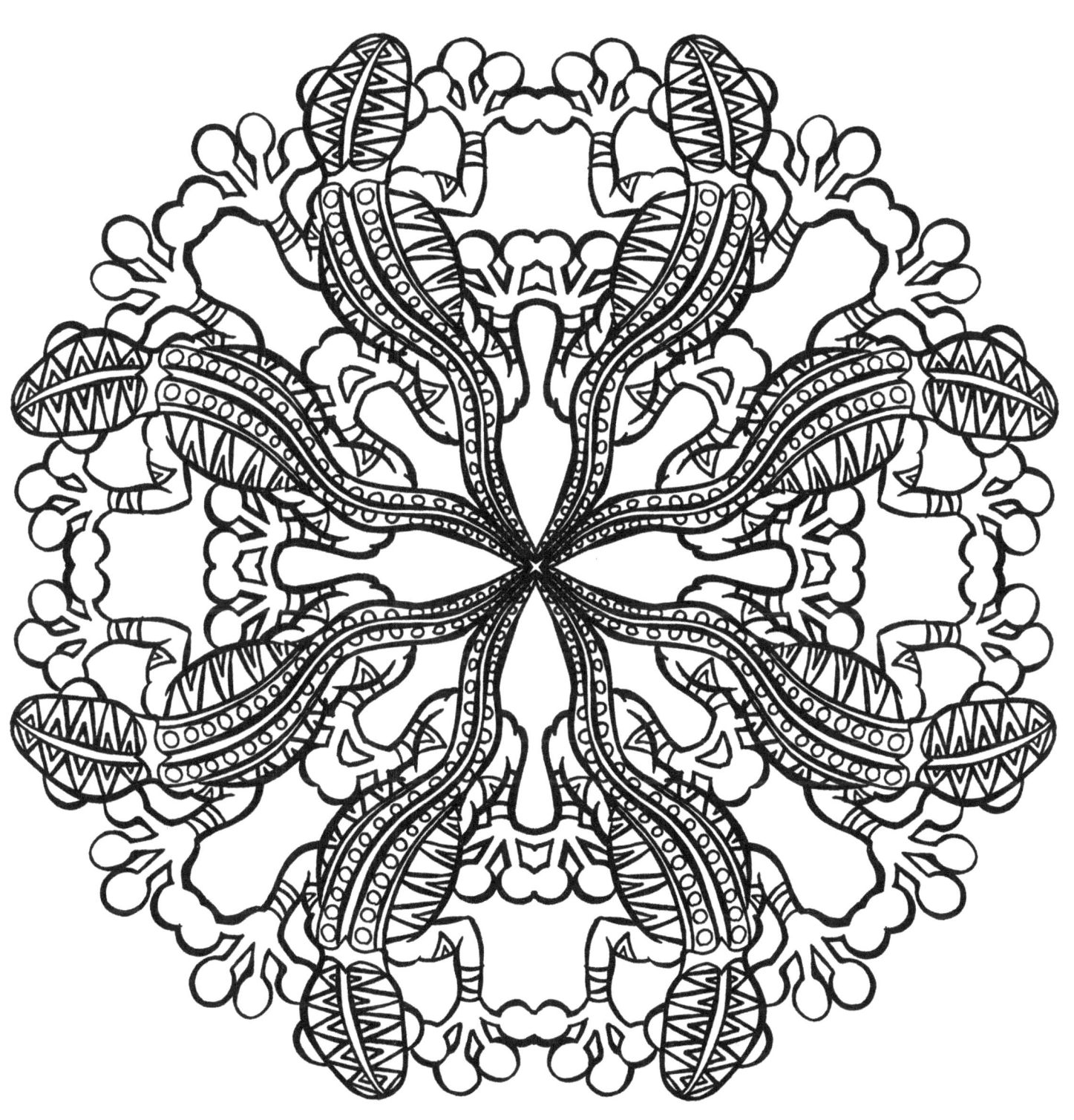

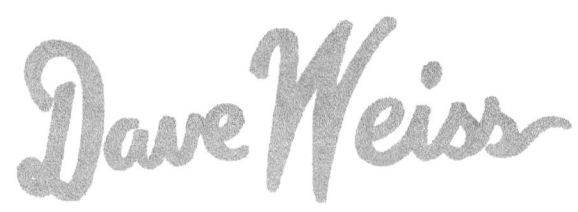

Kaleidoscopic Creatures Book 1
"Mondo Gekkos"

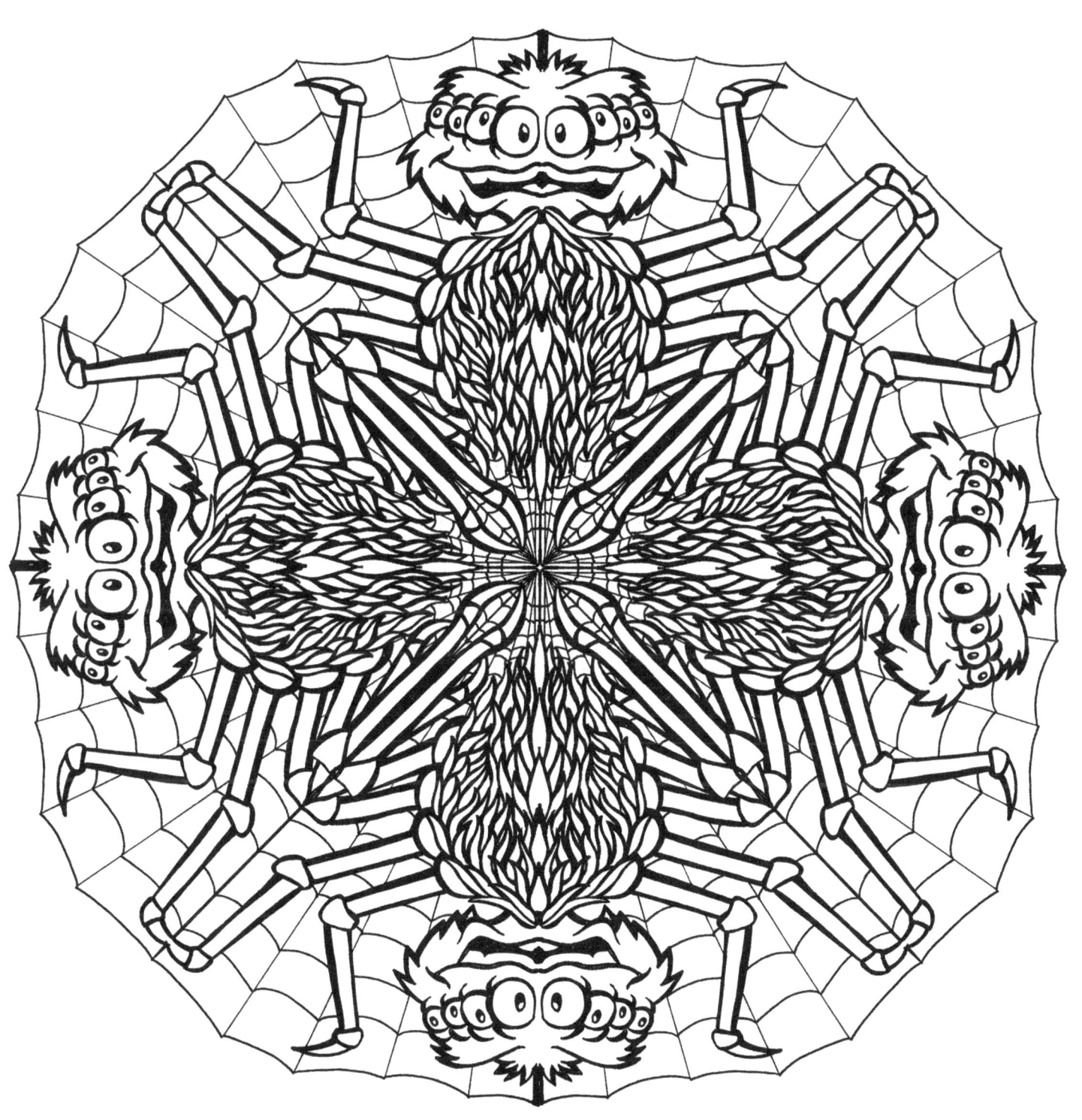

Dave Weiss

Kaleidoscopic Creatures Book 1
"A Tangled Web"

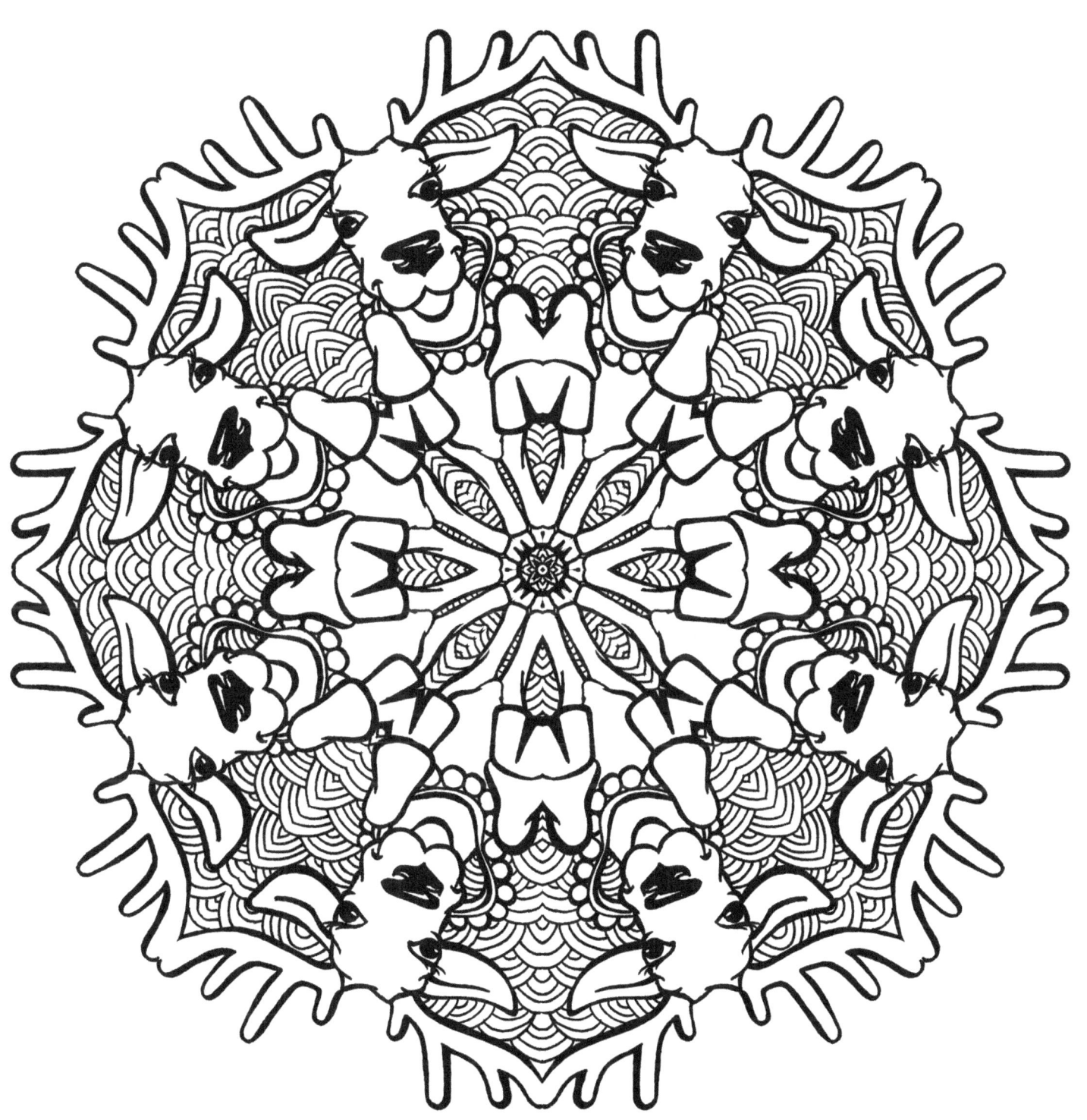

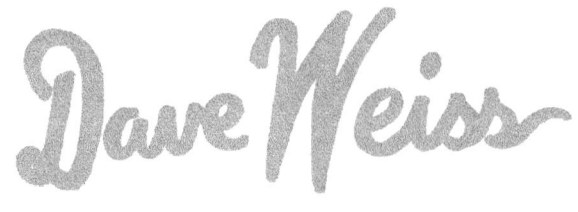

Kaleidoscopic Creatures Book 1
"Santa's 8"

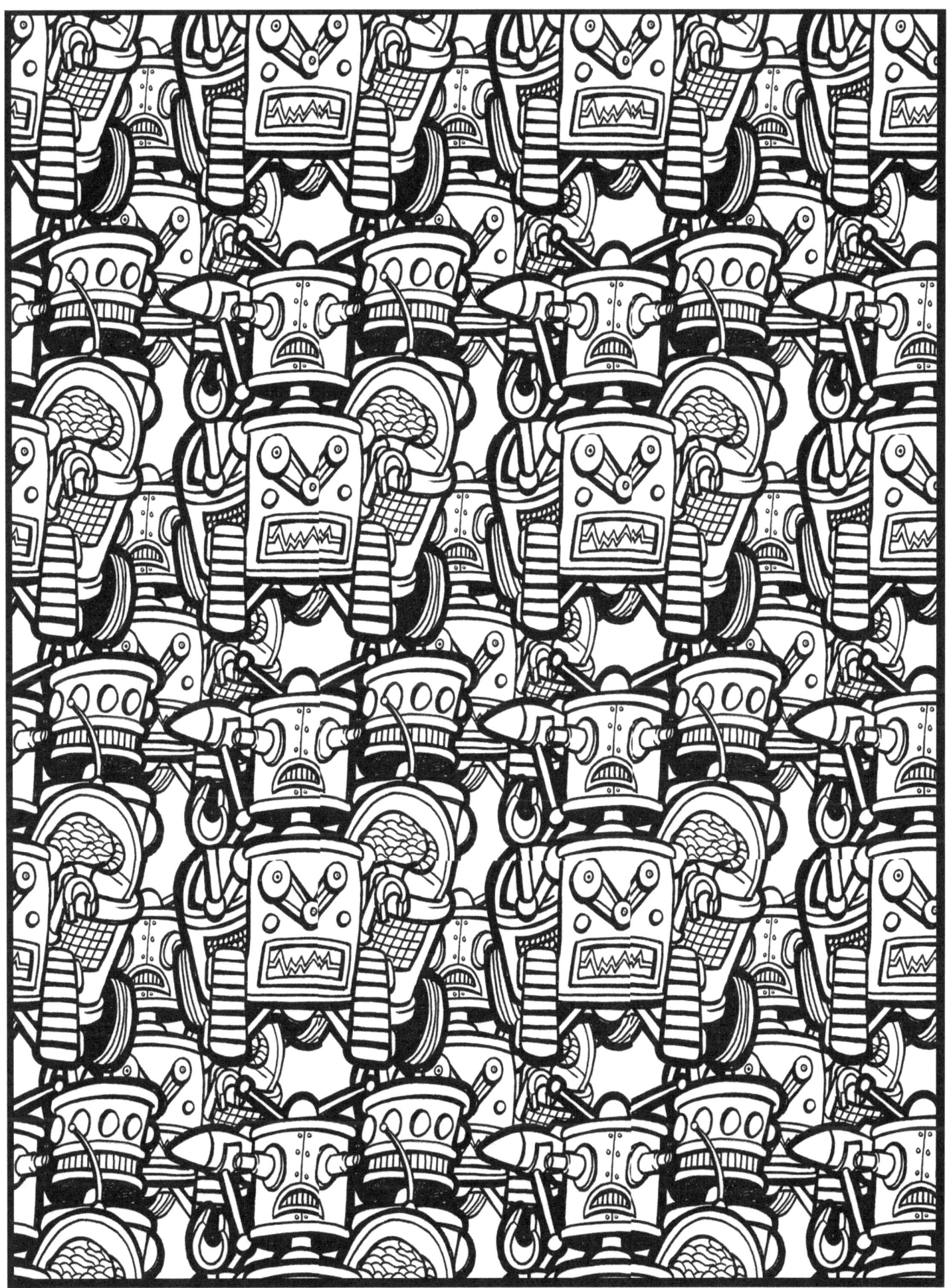

Dave Weiss

Kaleidoscopic Creatures Book 1
"We Robot"

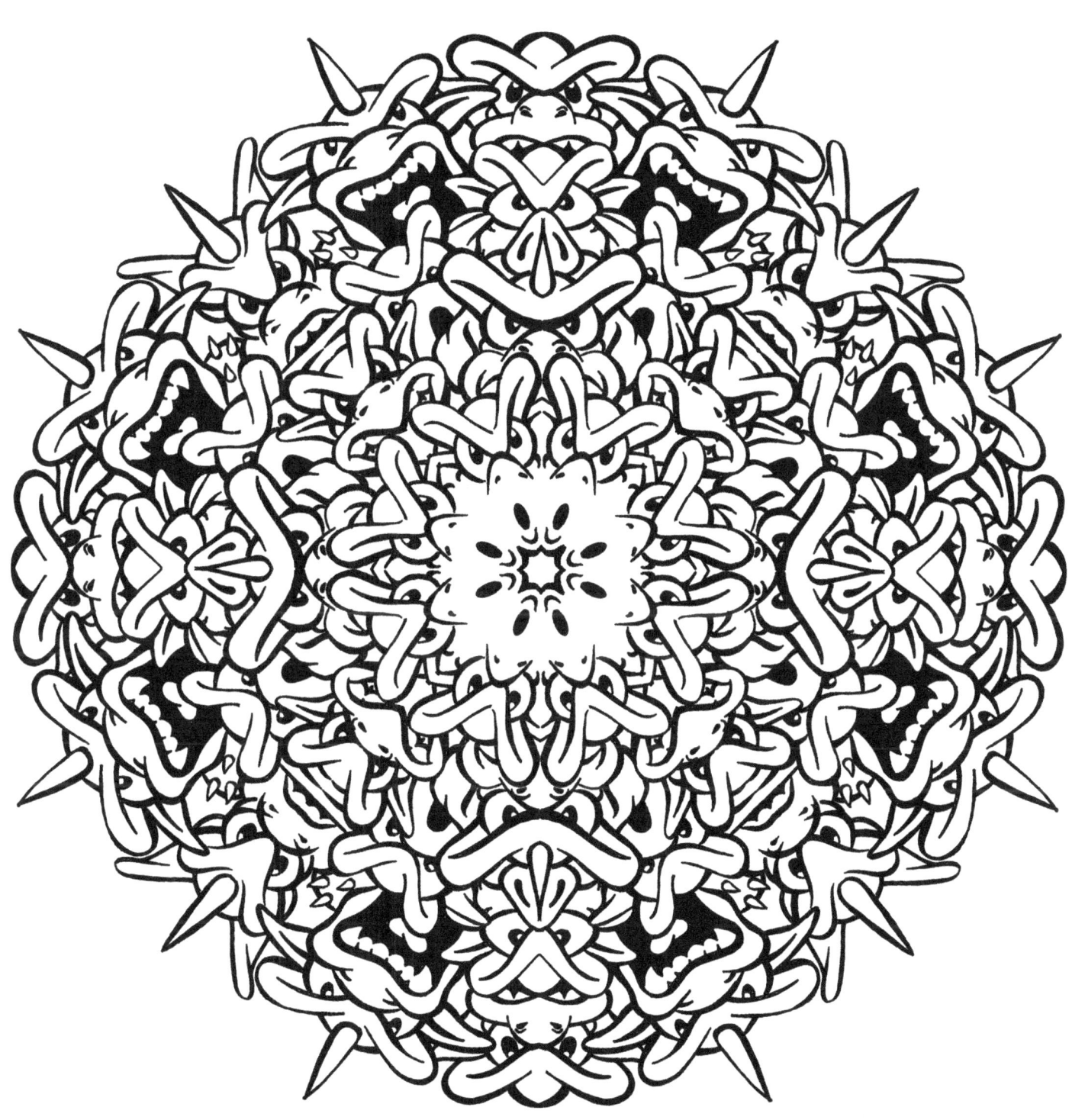

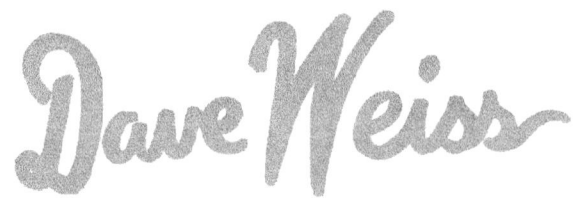

Kaleidoscopic Creatures Book 1
"Gobblin's"

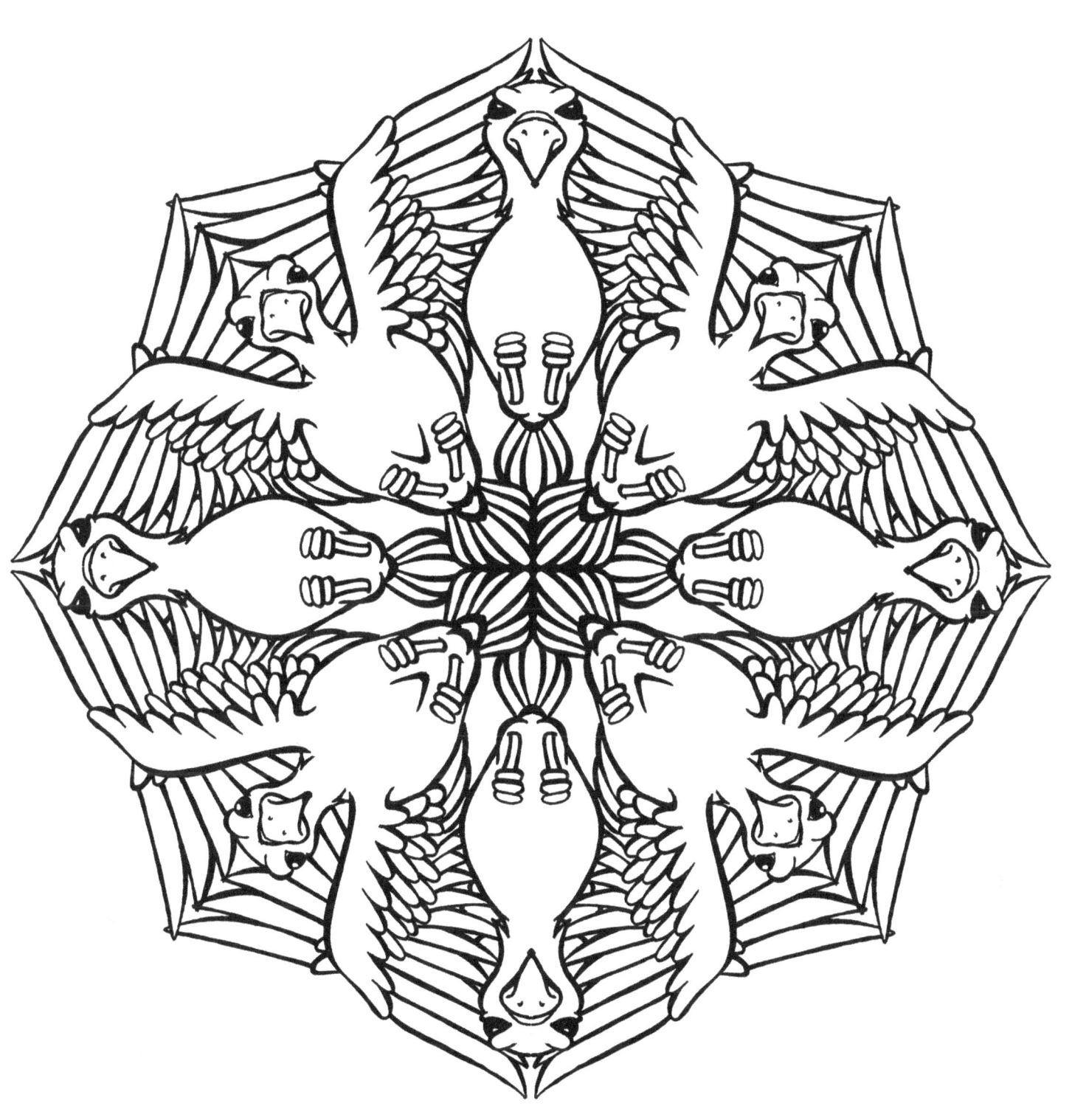

Dave Weiss

Kaleidoscopic Creatures Book 1
"Peace and Victory"

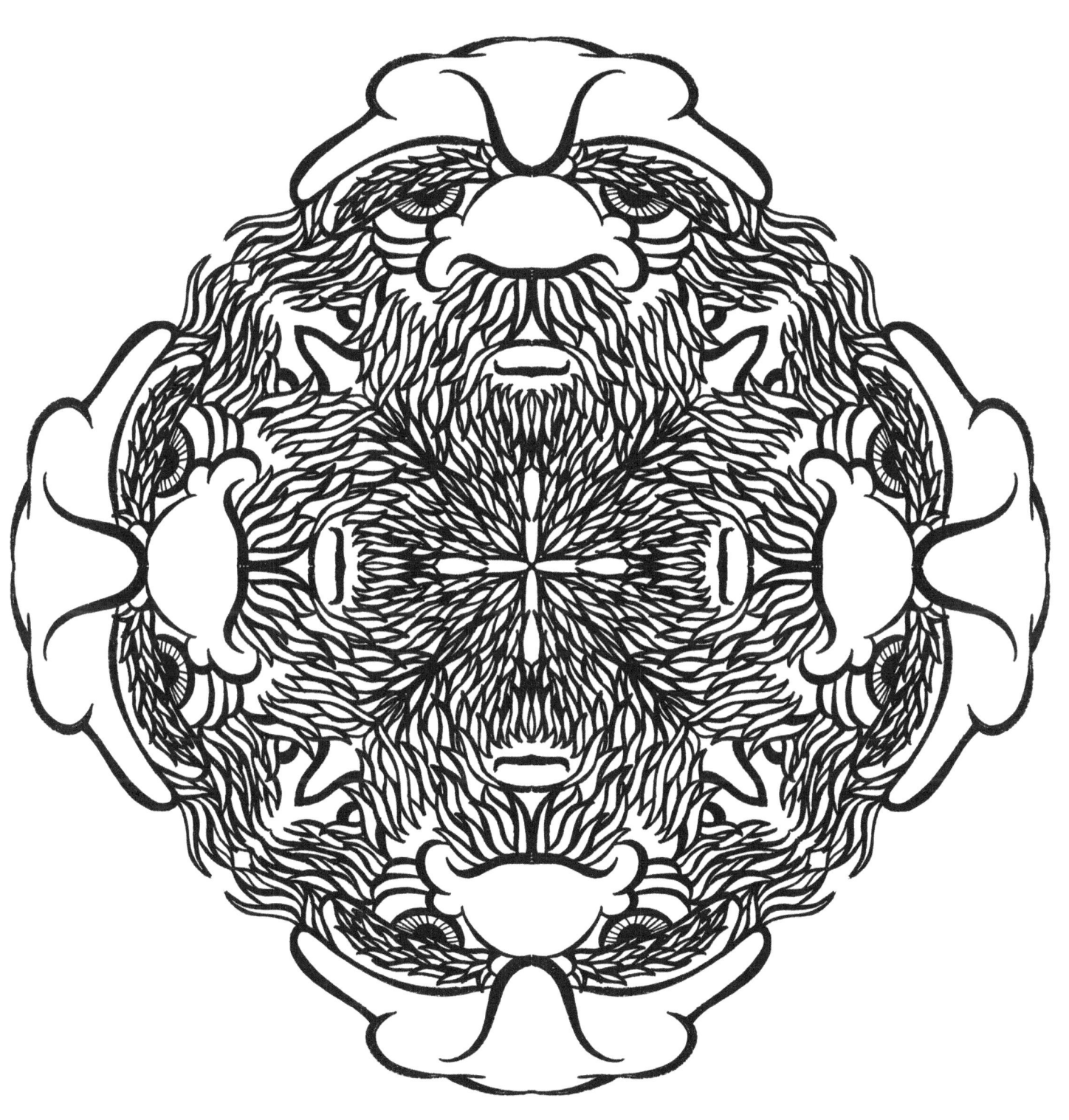

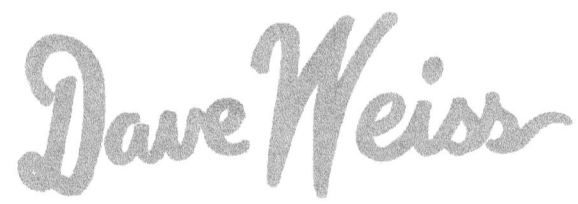

Kaleidoscopic Creatures Book 1
"G-Gnome"

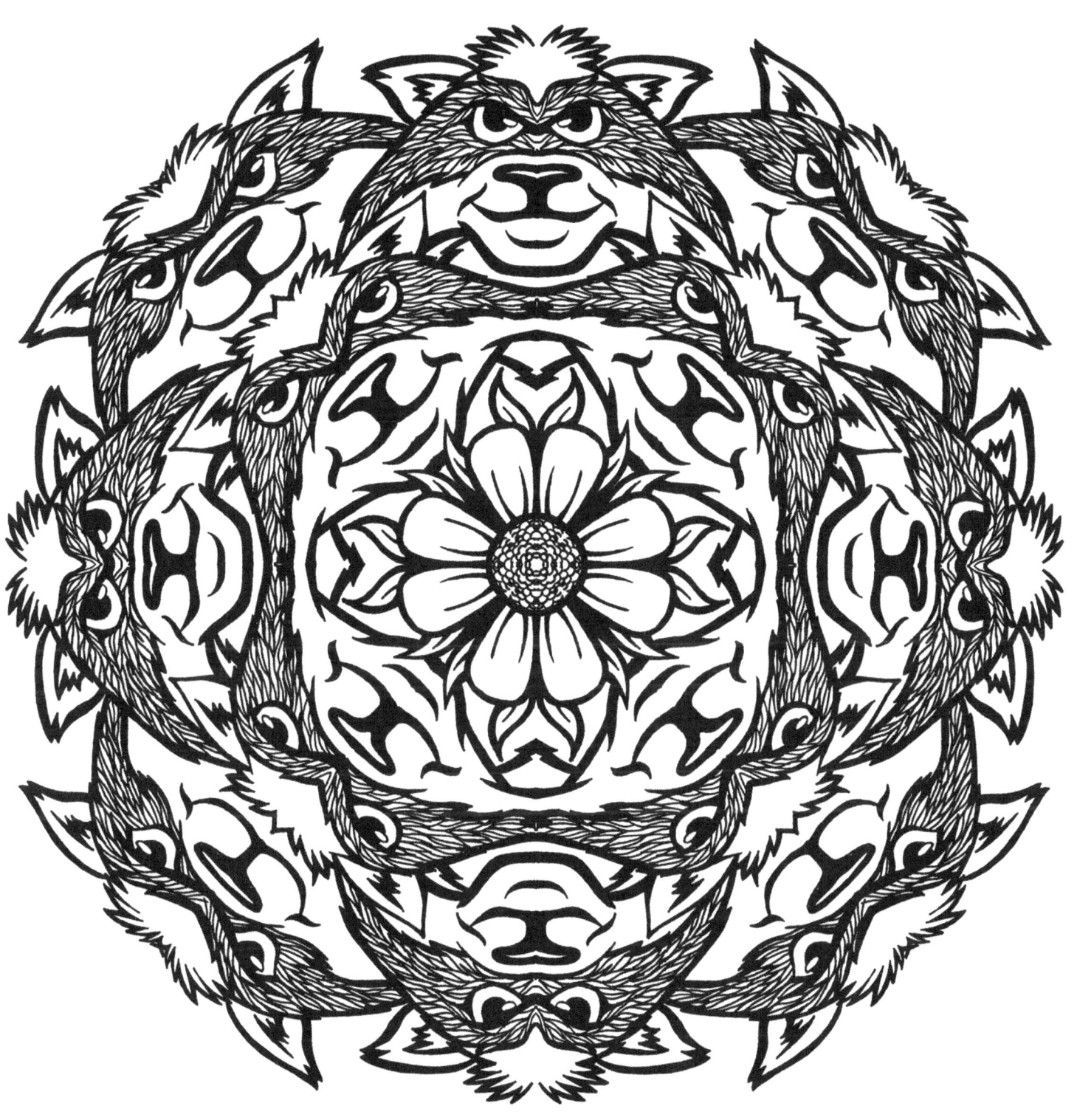

Dave Weiss

Kaleidoscopic Creatures Book 1
"'Cooncidence"

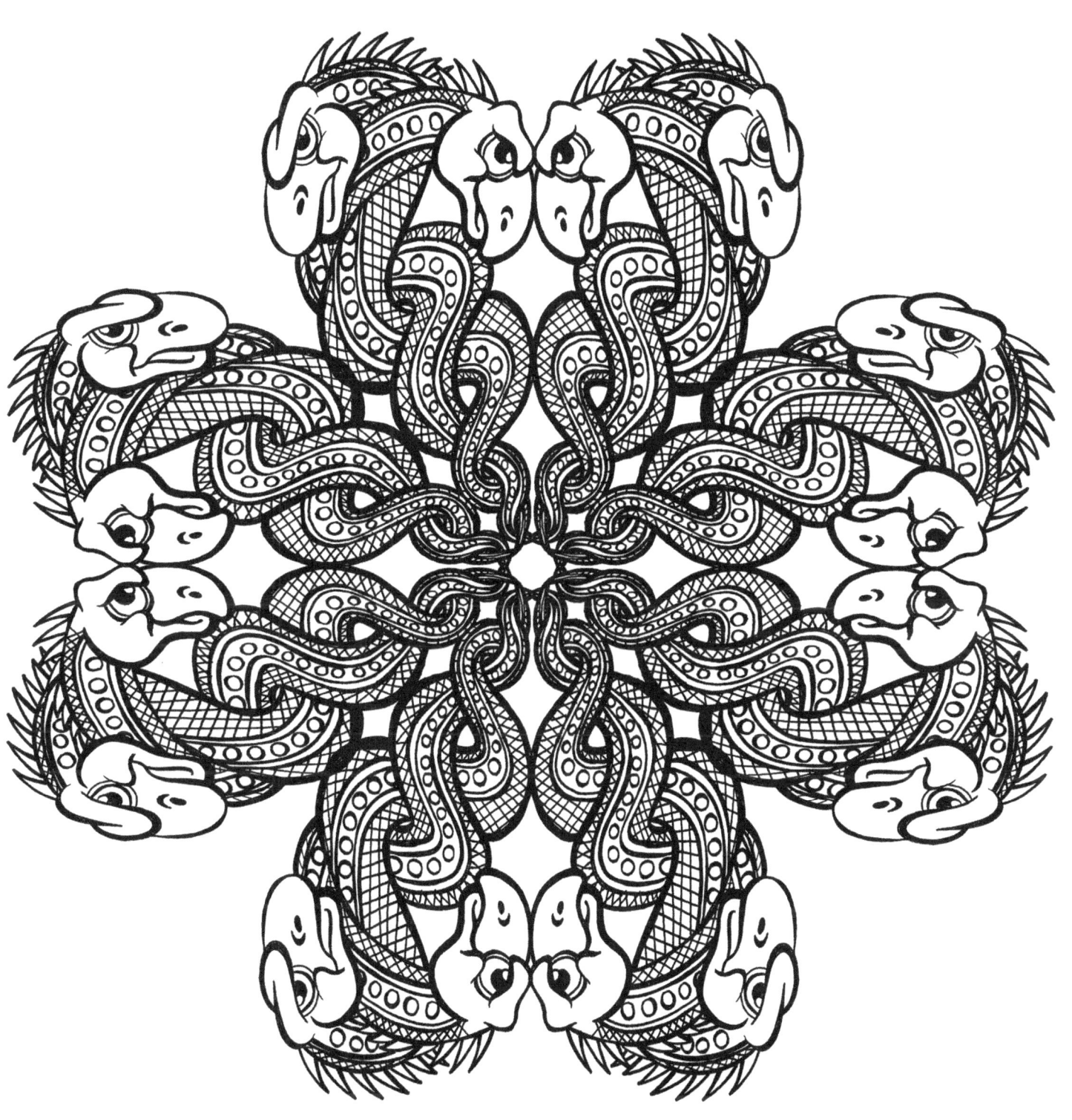

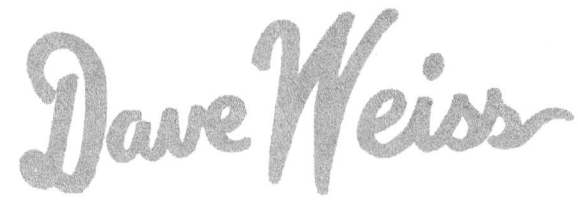

Kaleidoscopic Creatures Book 1
"Sea Serpents Intertwined"

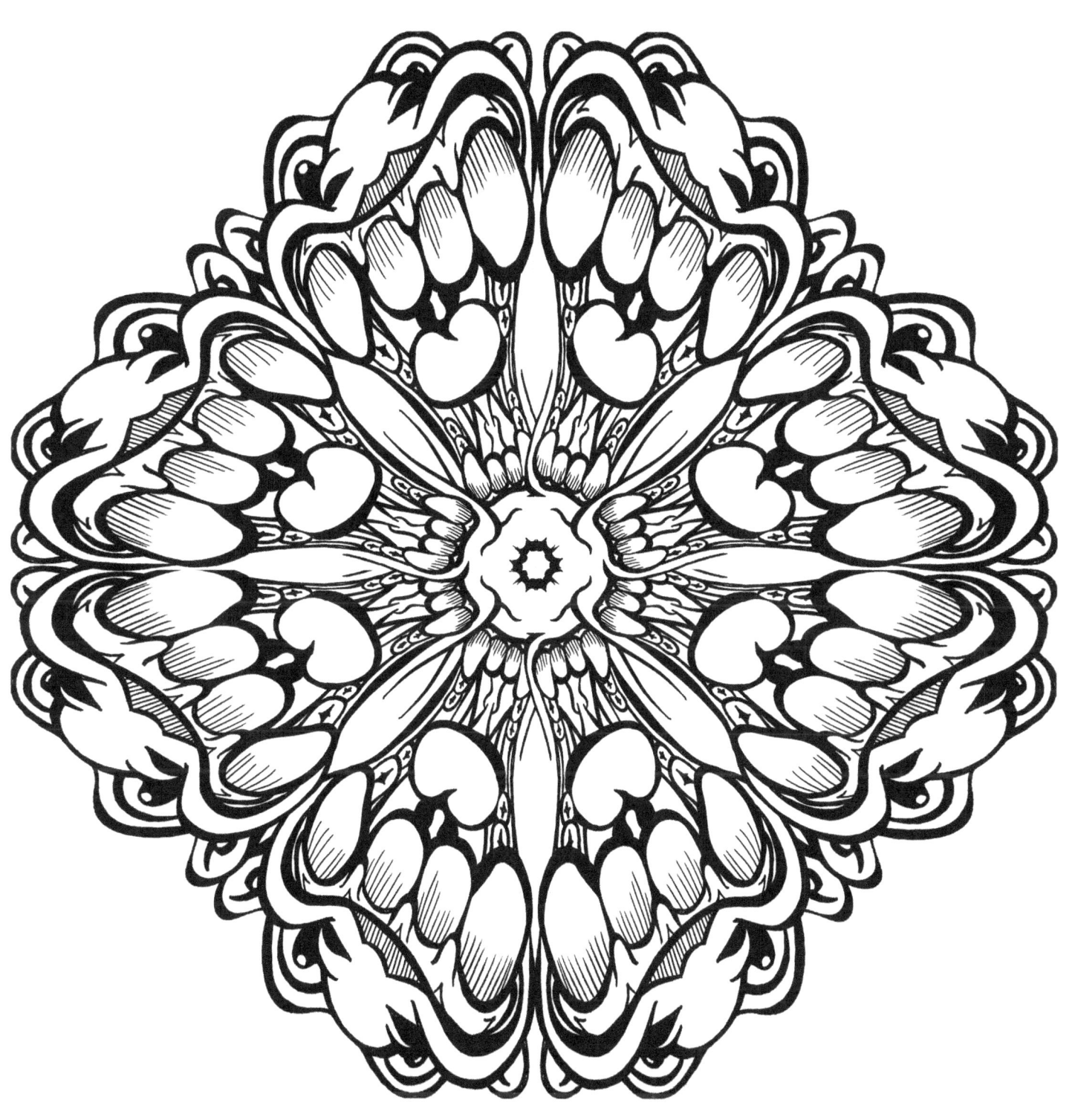

Dave Weiss

Kaleidoscopic Creatures Book 1
"Say Ah!"

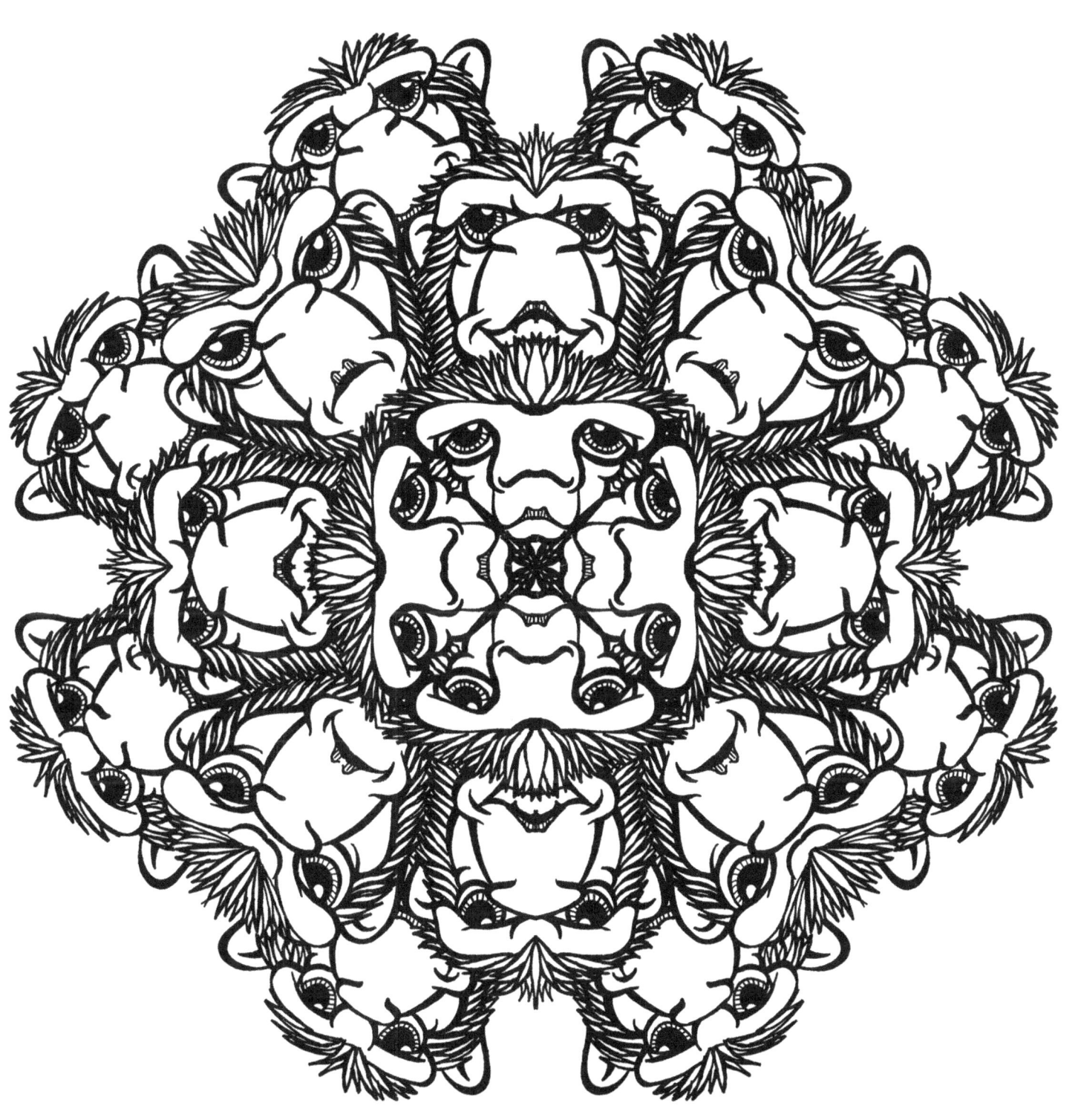

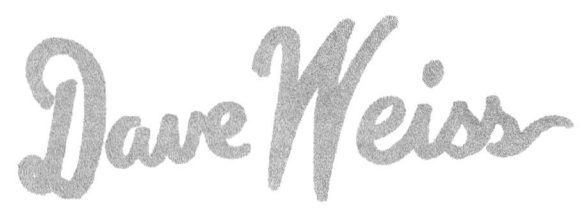

Kaleidoscopic Creatures Book 1
"Monkey Business"

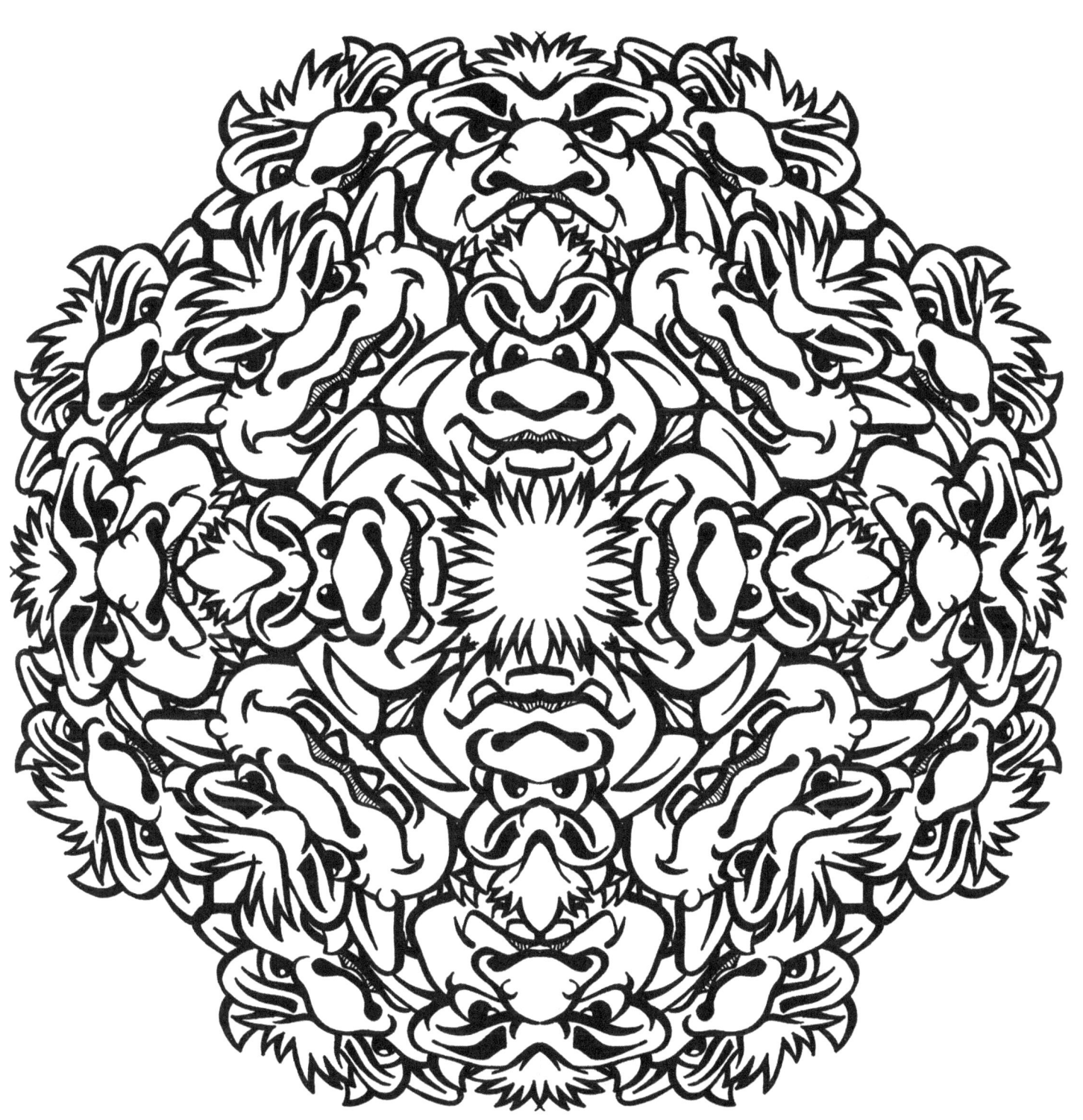

Dave Weiss

Kaleidoscopic Creatures Book 1
"Ogling Ogres"

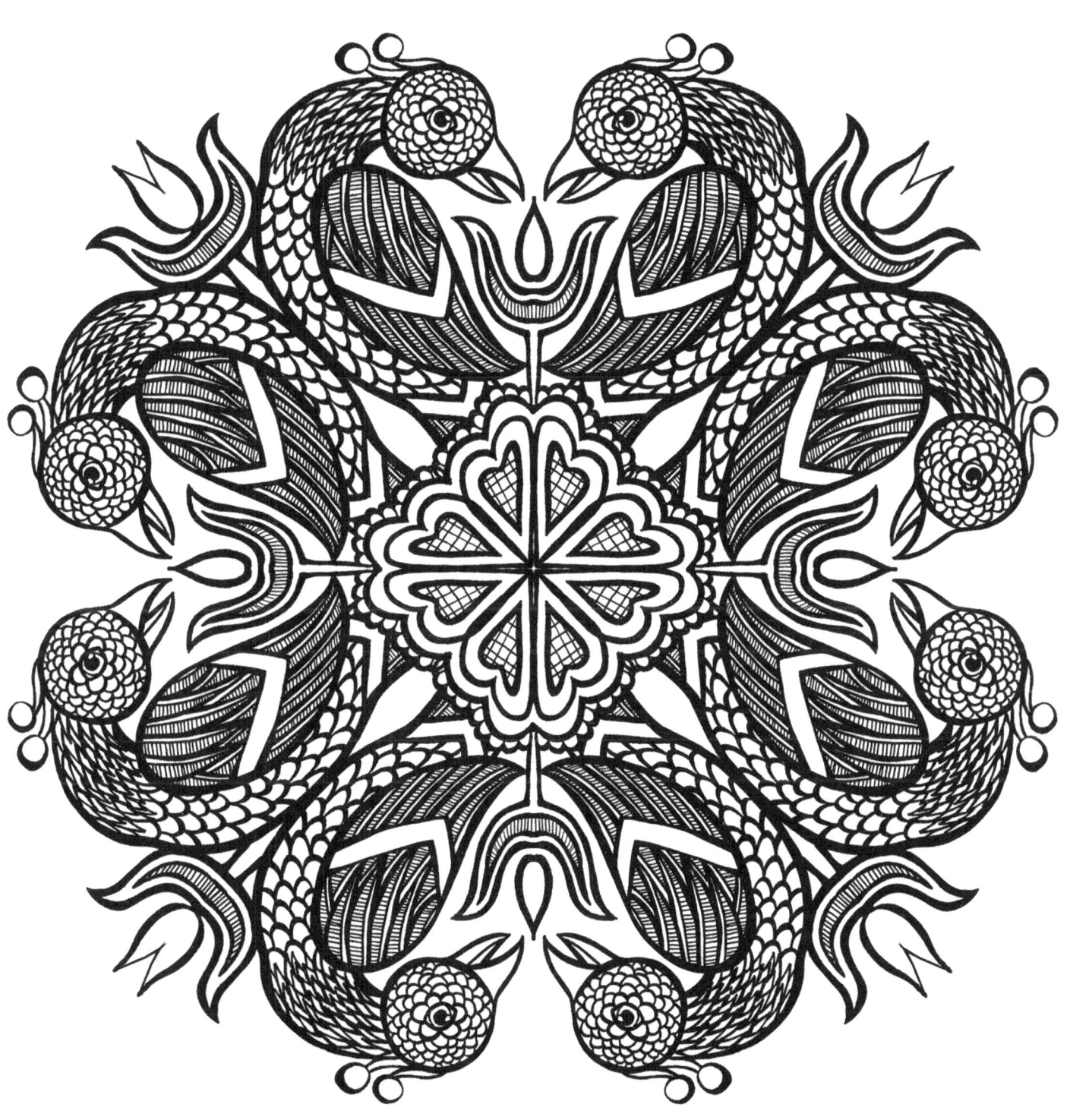

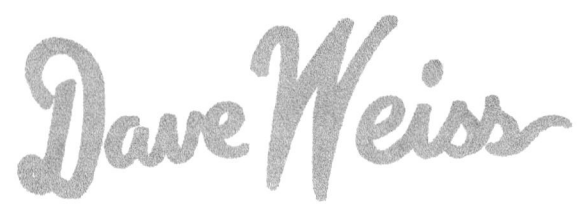

Kaleidoscopic Creatures Book 1
"Distlefink"

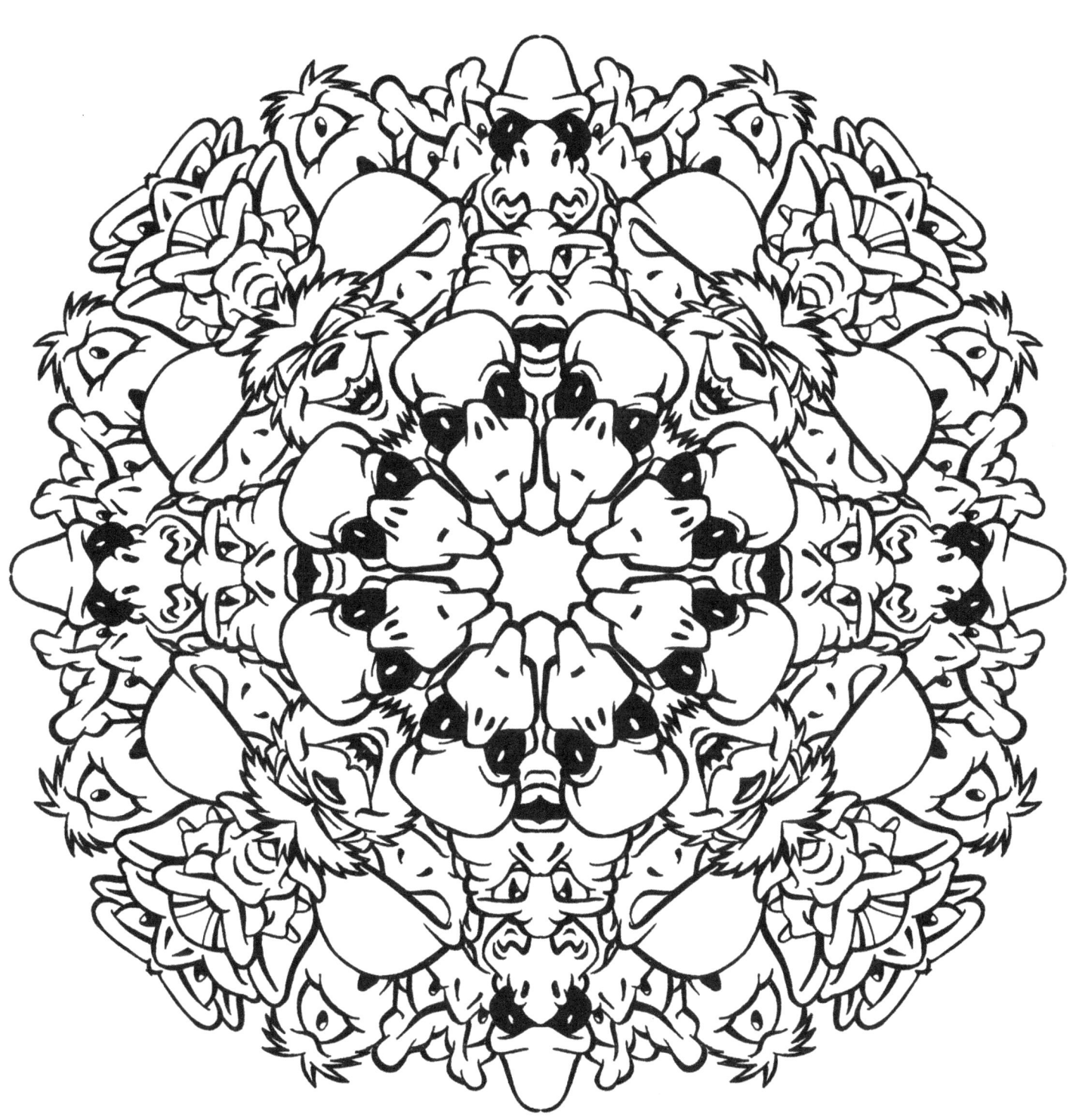

Dave Weiss

Kaleidoscopic Creatures Book 1
"Alien Nation"

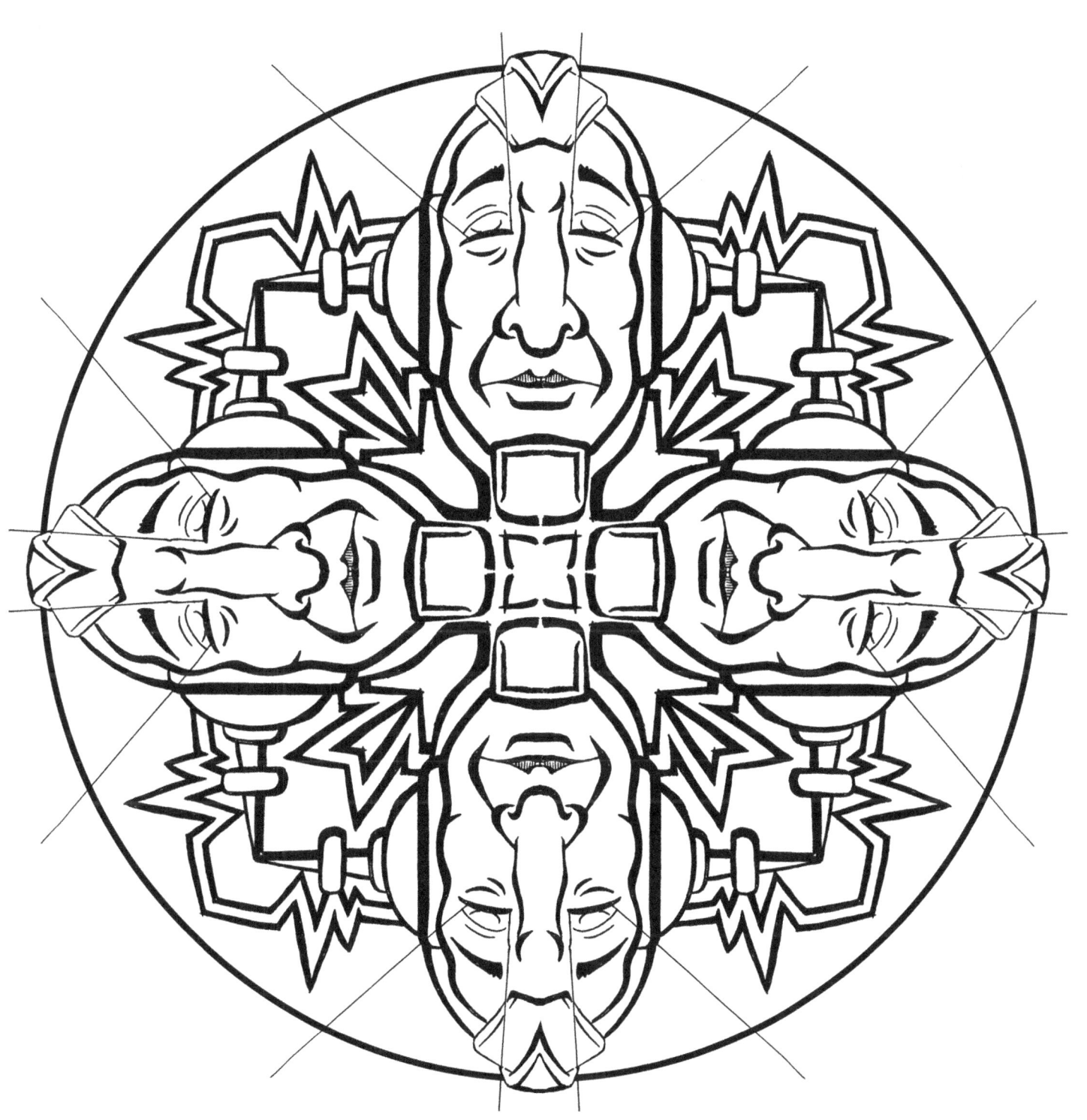

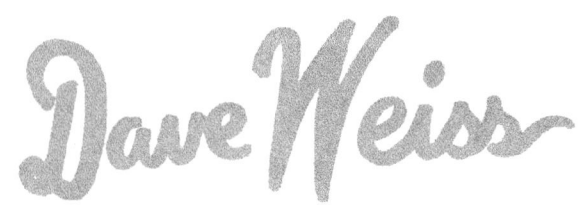

Kaleidoscopic Creatures Book 1
"Starship Trooper"

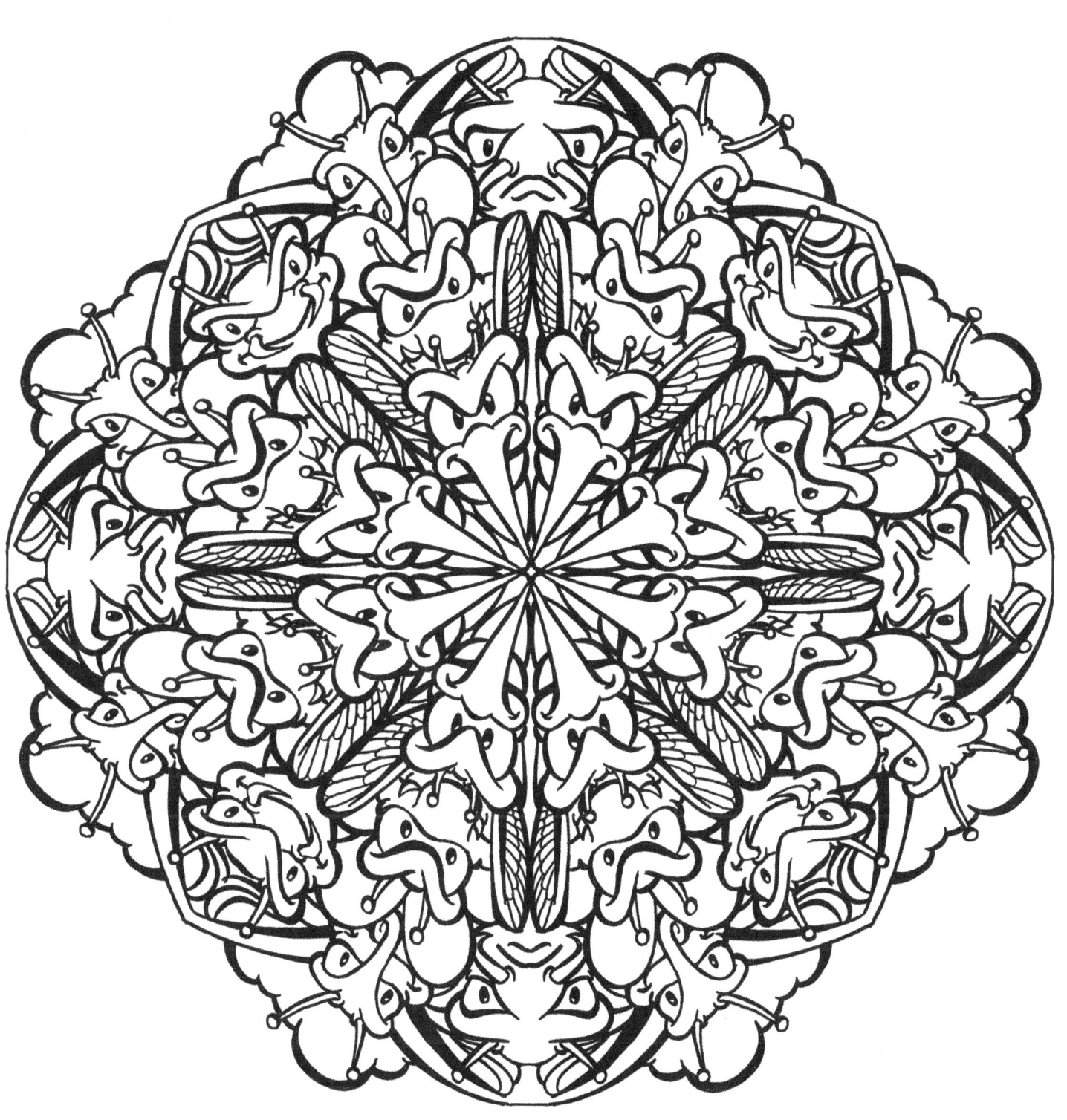

Dave Weiss

Kaleidoscopic Creatures Book 1
"Why Ya Buggin'?"

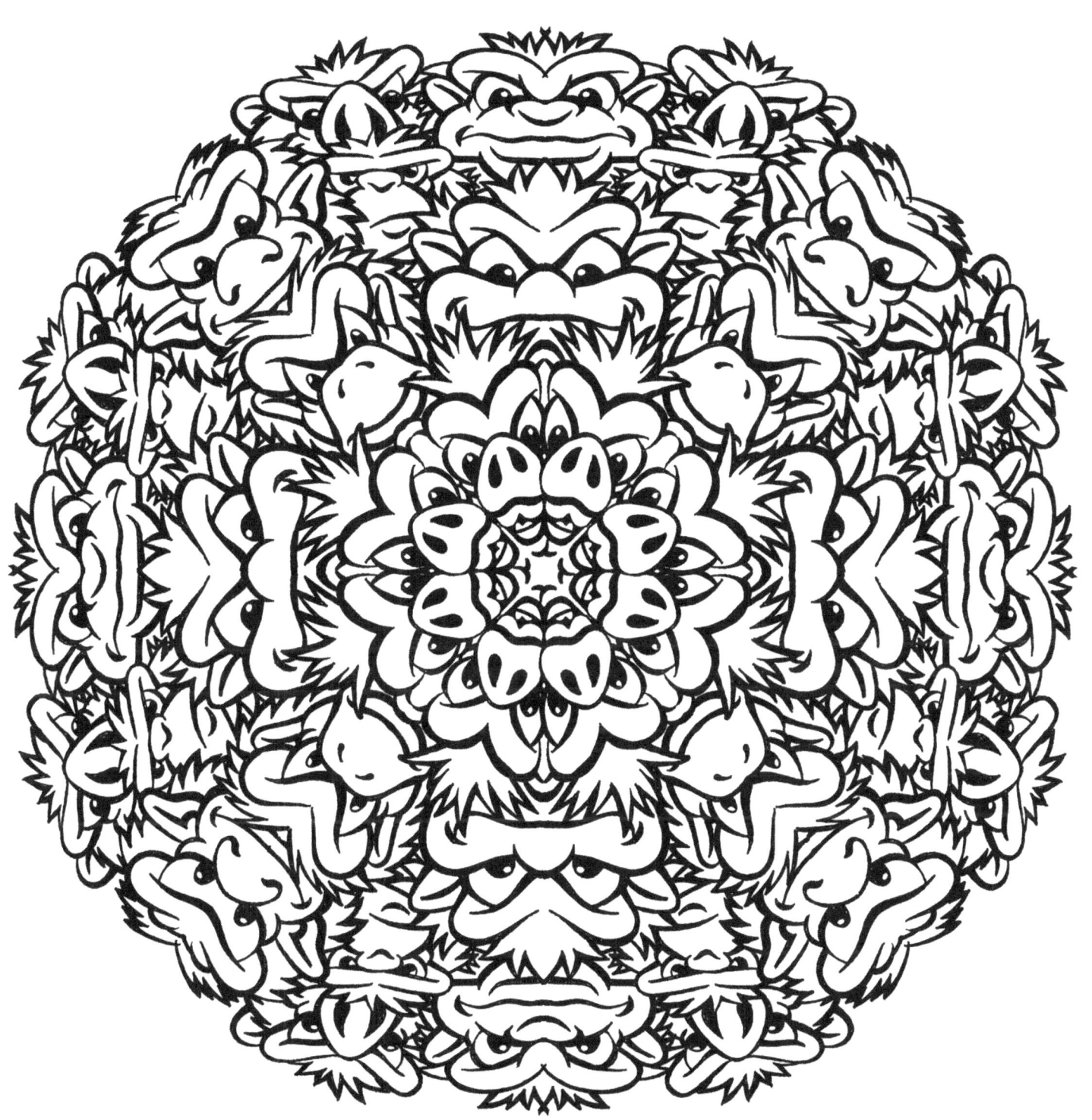

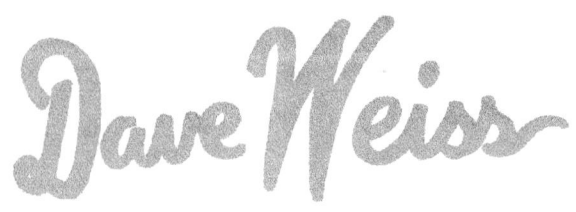

Kaleidoscopic Creatures Book 1
"Trollin'"

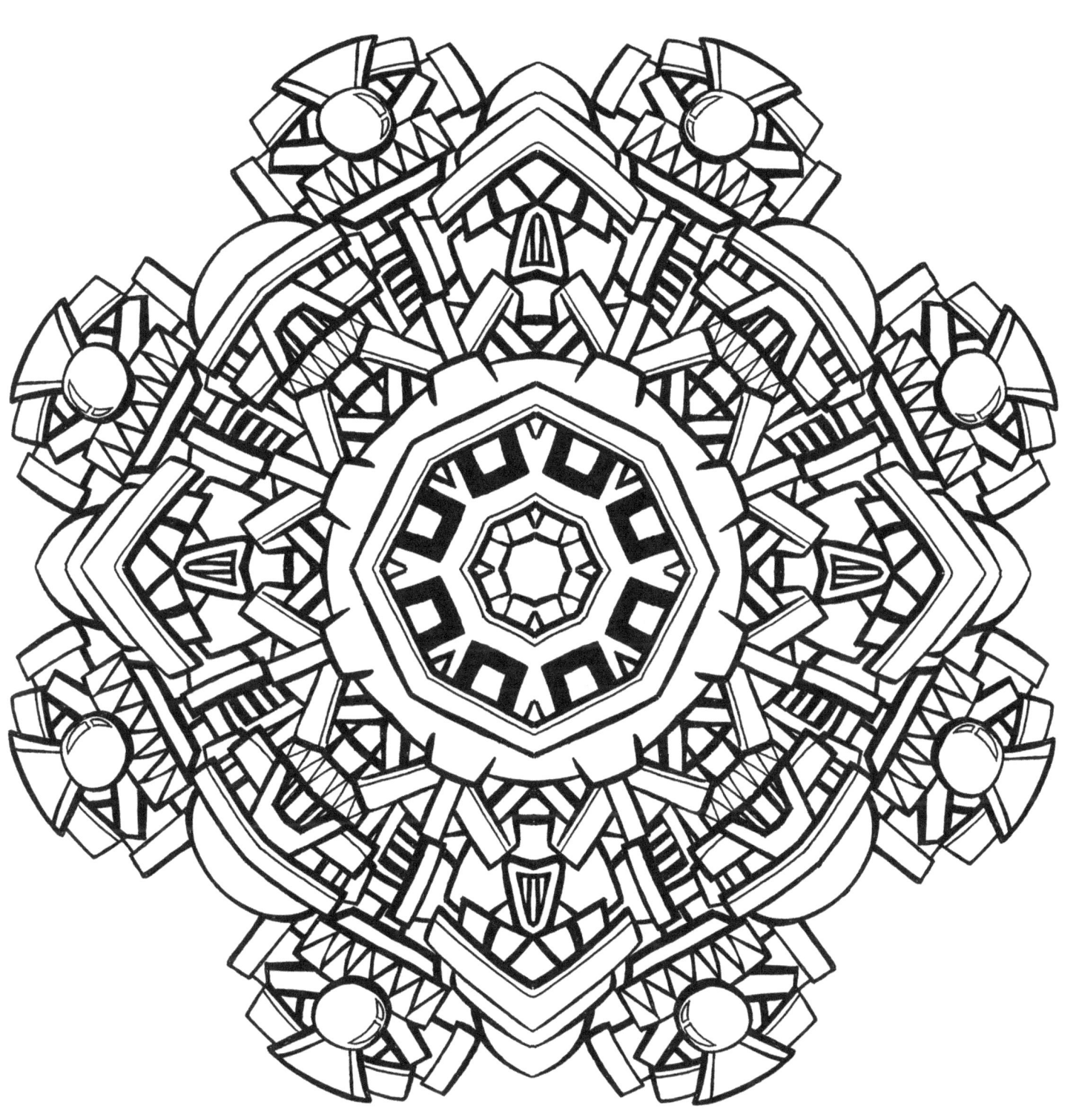

Dave Weiss

Kaleidoscopic Creatures Book 1
"Bots"

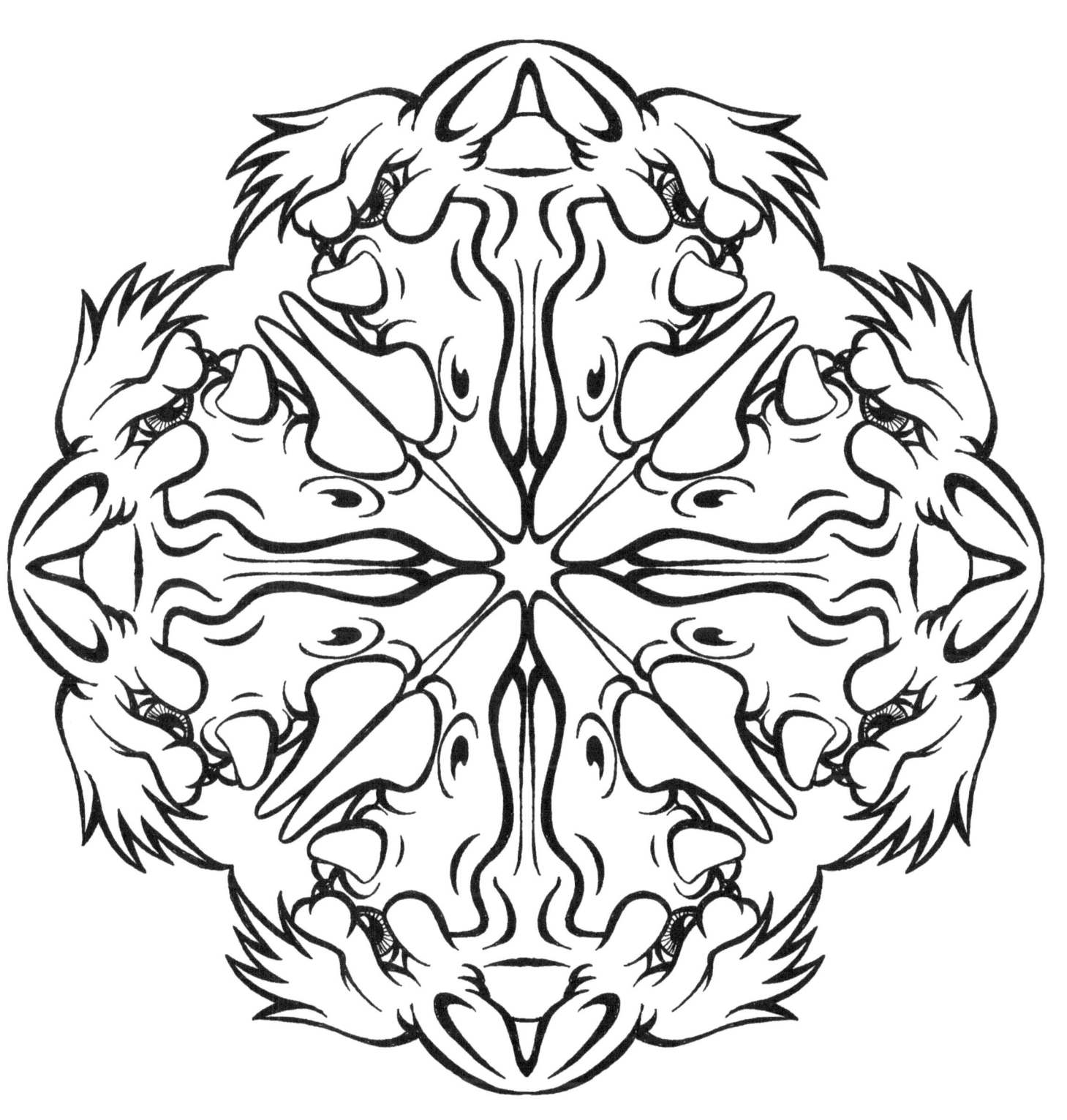

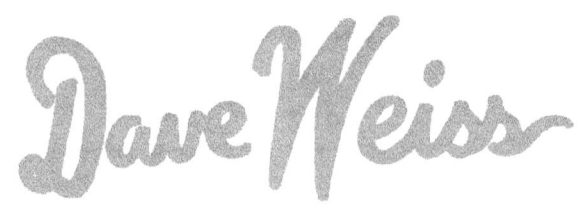

Kaleidoscopic Creatures Book 1
"Crash of Rhinos"

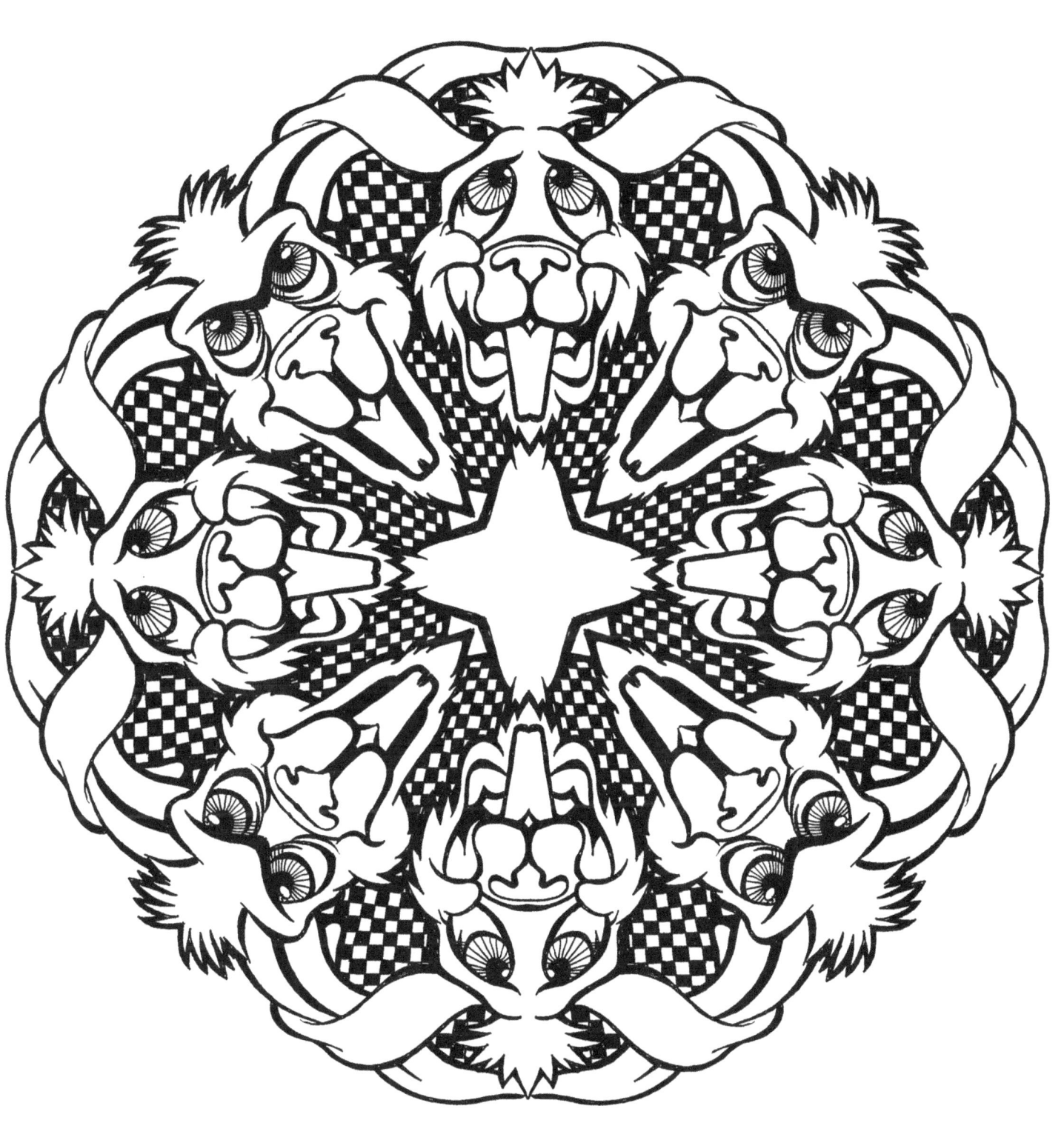

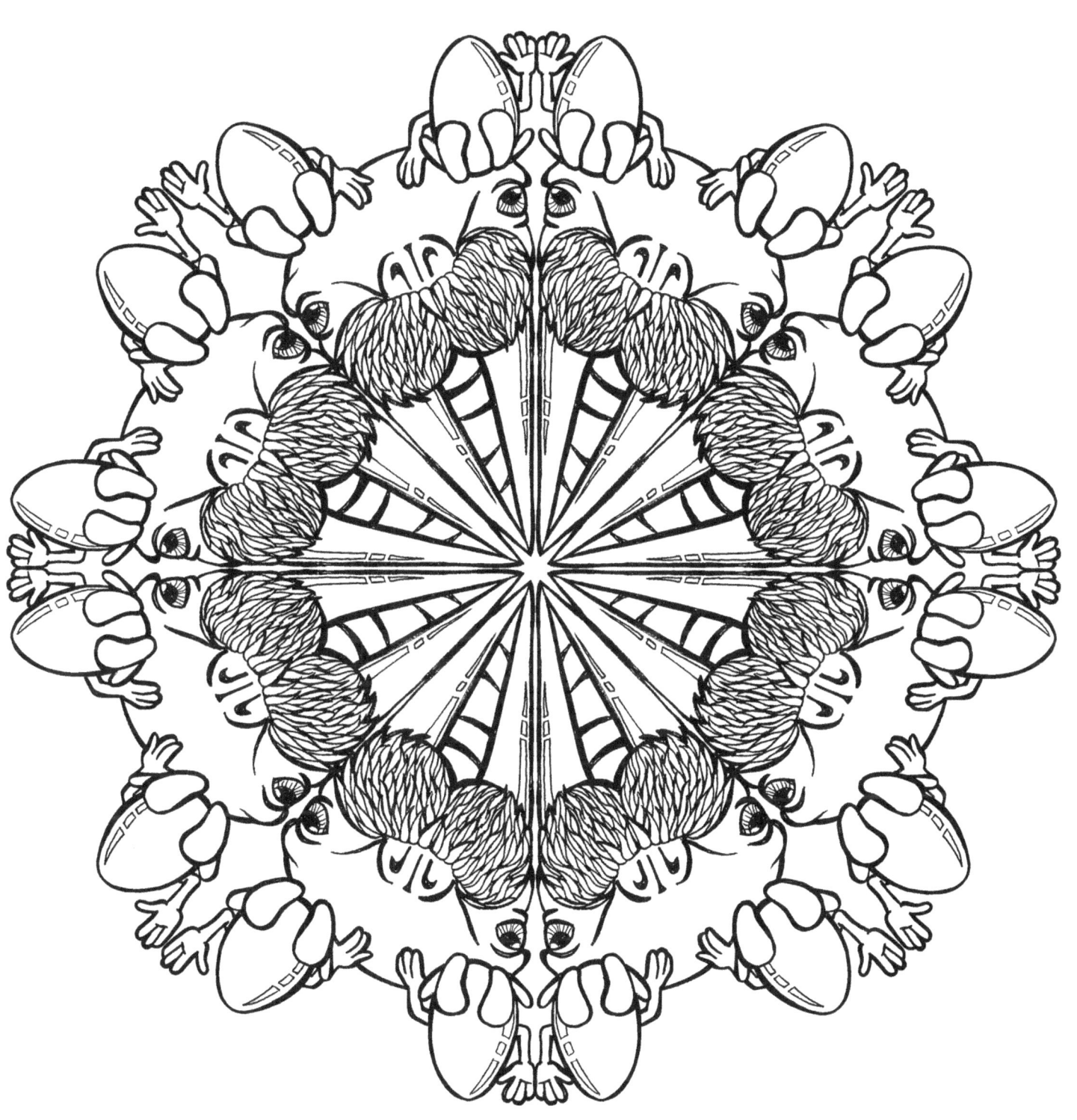

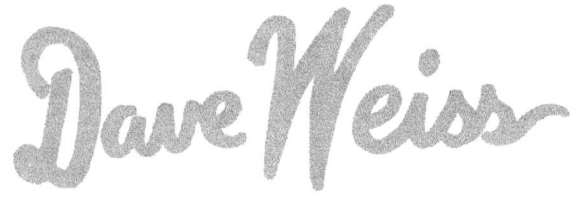

Kaleidoscopic Creatures Book 1
"I Am the Eggman, I am the
Walrus"

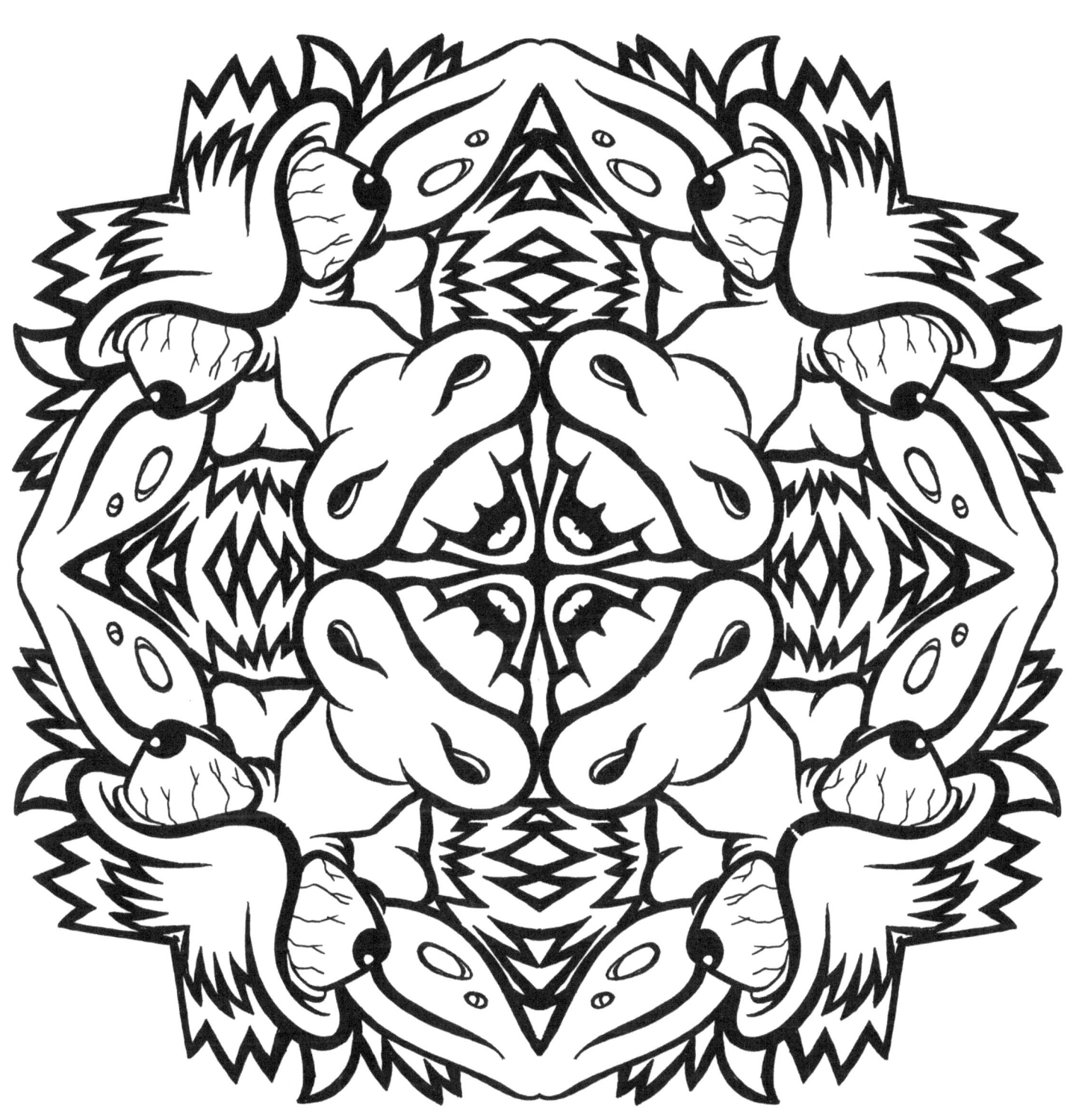

Dave Weiss

Kaleidoscopic Creatures Book 1
"Mad Cow"

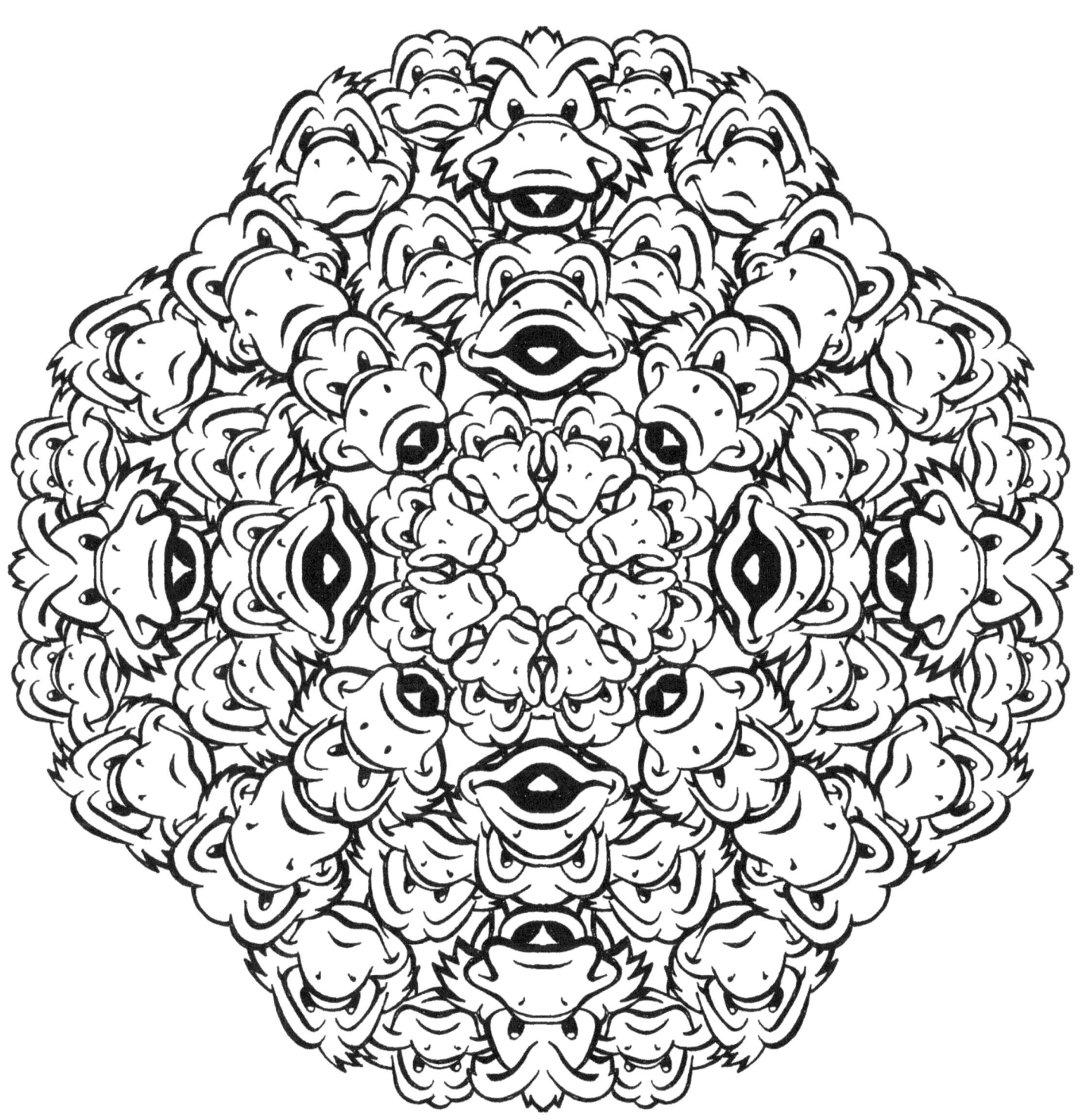

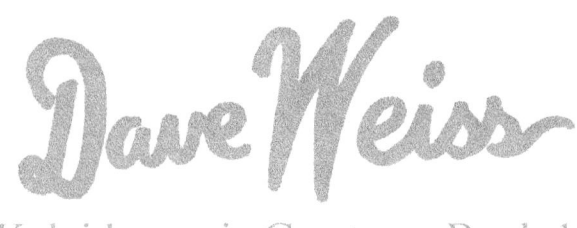

Kaleidoscopic Creatures Book 1
"Quackademia"

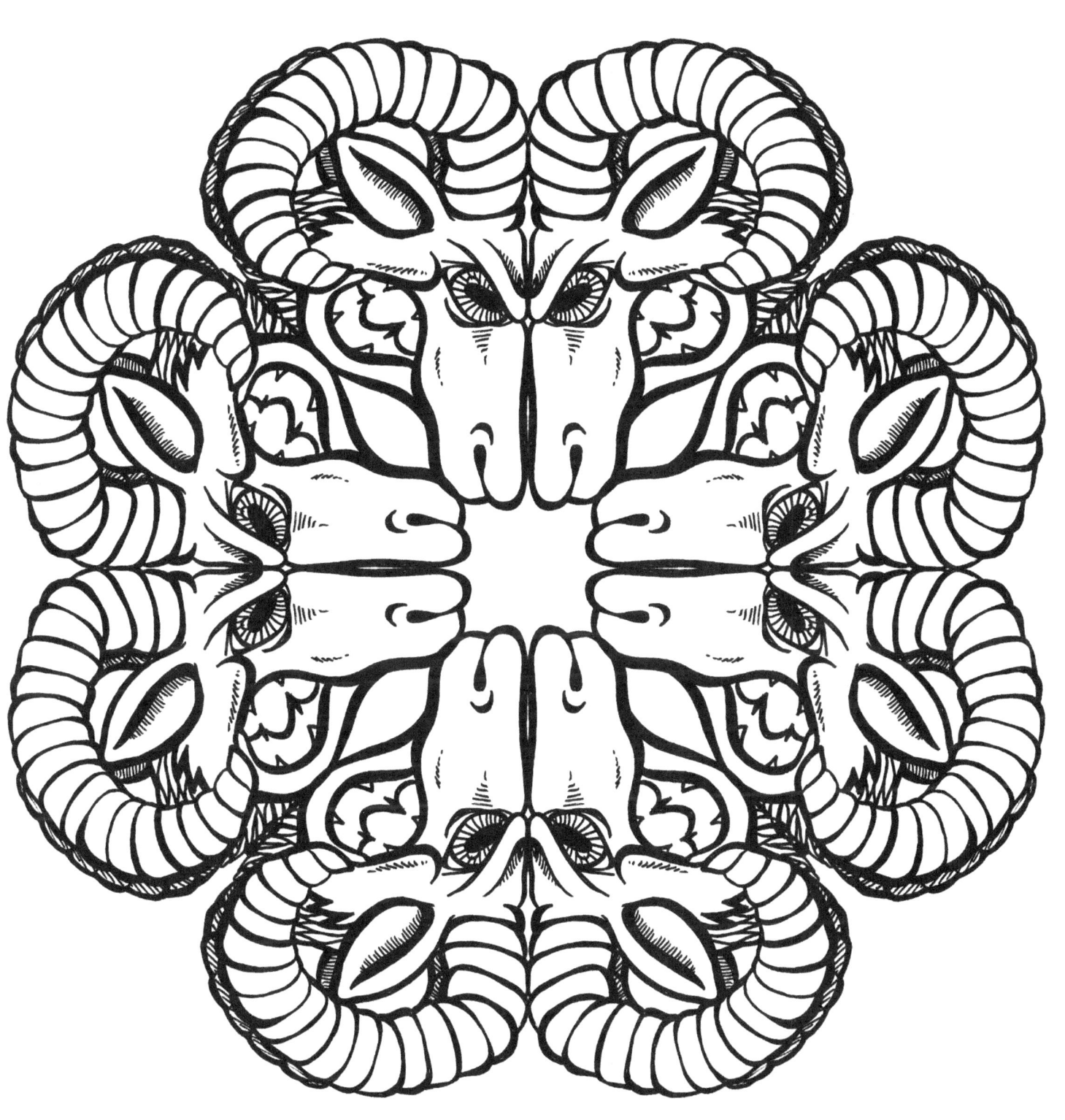

Dave Weiss

Kaleidoscopic Creatures Book 1
"Ram-Page"

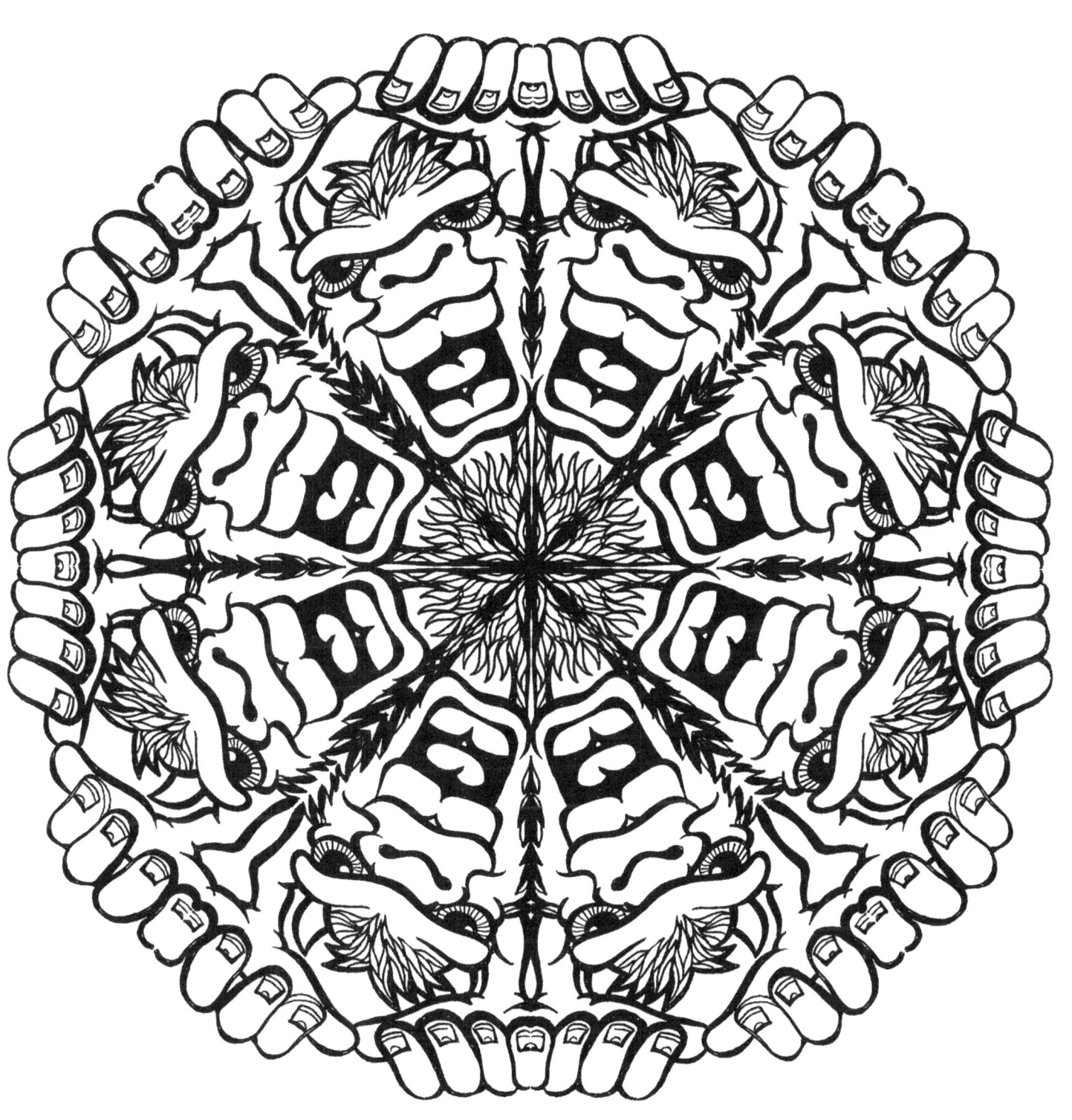

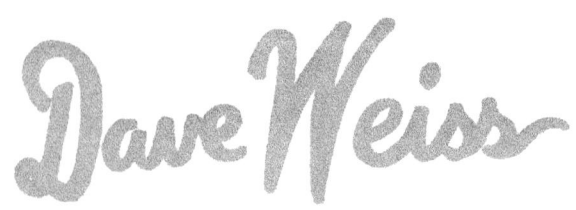

Kaleidoscopic Creatures Book 1
"Grabby Gabby"